CONTENTS

Introduction 4

The Nineteen-hundreds 6

The Nineteen-tens 21

The Trendy Twenties 39

The Threadbare Thirties 60

The Fighting Forties 78

The Fat Fifties 98

The Swinging Sixties 113

The Sinister Seventies 128

The Greedy Eighties 144

The Nostalgic Nineties 157

Epilogue 175

Introduction

History is horrible. Mainly because we have to learn it and then be tested on it.

Nobody ever teaches you the interesting things because you can't be tested on those. Nobody ever asks you, 'What did people laugh at a hundred years ago?' or, 'What made people cry? What did they read? What did they eat? What games did they play? Were teachers just as cruel?' No one ever answers when you ask vital questions like ...

These are the sort of things that help you understand what life was like for people in those days.

The history of this century *could* be just as boring as a history of the Middle Ages' monks. But it *should* be as interesting as your teacher's secret diary! It should be interesting because there are people who can still remember most of it ...

So, there are two ways of discovering the truth about the twentieth century. Ask someone really ancient who lived through it (a head teacher will usually do), or read a Horrible History of the Twentieth Century. And, by an amazing coincidence, that's just what you've started to do! Why not carry on?

The Nineteen-hundreds

In 1900 Queen Victoria is on the throne. She rules over the British Empire – 400 million people, almost a quarter of all the world's inhabitants. This makes the people of Britain rather proud, you understand. The English think they are the best of the Brits and some of them can be unbearable. Sir Claude Champion de Crespigny is typical. He says, 'Where there is a daring deed to be done in any part of the world, an Englishman should leap to the front to accomplish it.' In the next 100 years a lot of Brits will die believing that.

Timeline – 1900s

1900 Queen Vic's Empire covers 20 per cent of the earth's land surface – great for rich Brit businessmen, not so good for the poor. Coca-Cola goes on sale for the first time but the poor can't afford it. Brit Army at war with South African Boers. Lord Kitchener complains that the Boer enemy don't fight fairly because they move about rather than march in lines to be shot down by British machine-guns! The second modern Olympic games are held in Paris – and allow women to compete! How kind.

1901 Old Vic dies age 81. Family line up to kiss the dead queen's hand goodbye. Yeuch! New weapon against crime – the telephone! Call Whitehall 1212 for police help. Not many people have a phone, of course. (You can always

6

try shouting very loud instead.) Robert Falcon Scott sets off for the Antarctic to explore it for Britain. It will all end in tears (or icicles), of course, when he tries to reach the Pole in 11 years' time…

1902 Foul football match in Glasgow. England play Scotland. The score is 200 dead when a stand collapses. Meanwhile Scotland's worst poet, William McGonagall, dies. His greatest successes are forgotten, like his advert for Sunlight Soap …

> You can use it with great
>   pleasure and ease,
> Without wasting any elbow
>   grease;
> And, when washing the most
>   dirty clothes,
> The sweat won't be dripping
>   from your nose.

1903 British police fight crime with a new weapon … fingerprints! Over in the USA the Wright brothers fly the first aeroplane. Some people don't think this flying thing will catch on. The first Teddy Bears are made in America and named after President Teddy Roosevelt – who refused to shoot a cuddly little bear cub. (What a nice man, you'd think – unless you happened to be a fully grown bear, of course.)

1904 Police have to fight a new crime – cars speeding at over 20 m.p.h. – and the police are armed with stopwatches. Motorists fight back with a new organisation, the AA (Automobile Association). Women start to get tough because they can't vote in elections. They form 'suffragette' groups, embarrass the government and the law, and go to jail. *Peter Pan* play first shown. An event called *Plunging* is held at the Olympics – dive in and float as far as possible in one minute. Weird!

1905 Lady Blount is the leader of the Zetetic Society and publishes magazines from her home in Surrey. Her great achievement is to prove, once and for all, what we all know. In 1905 she proves that the Earth is flat! A survey shows that three out of four women have to beg their husbands for money.

1906 Tennis player May Sutton shocks Wimbledon when she appears in a short dress and *no corsets underneath!* Meanwhile the *Daily Mail* newspaper argues that those suffragette women shouldn't have the vote because 'women know nothing about politics'. The suffragettes in Holloway prison protest by refusing to eat Christmas dinner. (They would be too polite to say 'Stuff your turkey', of course.)

1907 Shock report. Too many children

are smoking. Some doctors say it's 'probably harmless', so that's all right. (Cigarette-makers are still saying that over 100 years later!) The first soap powder is made with *perborate* and *silicate* – so it's called, guess what? Per-Sil ... Persil!

1908 A new law says that children under 14 years old can no longer be sent to adult prisons. But they can go to their very own prisons, known as Borstals. (And really wicked children could be punished by making them go to school!) The first horror film, *Doctor Jekyll and Mr Hyde,* is shown at British cinemas. At least twenty more versions of this film are made during the twentieth century. First vacuum cleaners go on sale – very expensive and only for the servants of the very rich. First School Doctors Report says (about nits) there are cases where, 'the whole head appeared to be moving with vermin!' (So why not simply sack the Head?)

1909 Parliament grants the first old age pensions but they're just 25p. (Not worth grovelling to Granny for.) MPs in parliament give themselves £8 a week. A Frenchman is the first person to fly over the English Channel. Police hunt down criminals on their new vehicles ... bicycles!

9

Potty poems

Imagine a world without television, internet, games consoles or even radio! How were people entertained? The entertainers couldn't come into your house through that screen in the corner. So you would have to go out to the entertainers. There were plays and musicals and pantomimes and concerts held in theatres in most towns.

Sometimes the shows were a mixture of music and drama and magicians and jugglers and acrobats and comedians. These mixed shows were known as Music Hall. The Music Hall had been enjoyed in Victorian times but something new became popular in the 1900s. Poetry.

Actors, actresses, singers and comedians began to put story poems into their Music Hall acts. Some were dramatic stories like the one about the stagecoach driver, Bill, who promised to deliver the cargo of gold safely and fought off an armed gang ...

> *The boys rushed out with lanterns, and found Bill*
> *   there in the seat*
> *Held by the rawhide picket rope, the gold chest safe*
> *   at his feet.*
> *He'd fought his fight to the finish, although he was*
> *   riddled with lead.*
> *He'd given his word – and he'd kept it –*
> *He'd driven for three hours ... dead!*

By Callum and Clarke, 1918

Some were tragic …

Performed by Bransby Williams, 1910

some were hilarious …

> *Nell was a diver's daughter –*
> *He used to dive under the ships.*
> *He'd walk on the bed of the ocean*
> *And tread on the fishes and chips.*

Performed by Billy Bennett, 1926

and some were romantic …

> *Through falling in love I've had lots of surprises,*
> *I've flirted with girls of all sorts, shapes and sizes;*
> *My first love affair was a bad one I'm told,*
> *I think at the time I was eighteen months old . . .*

Performed by Bransby Williams, 1921

But people like you have always been entertained by *horrible* stories. This 1906 poem was written to be performed on stage. Don't read it if you have …
1 Nightmares
2 Common sense.

The 11:69 Express
By Ronald Bagnall and William S. Robinson (1906)

*You'll want a railway story while you wait for
the London train,
It's a story I've never told yet, so I'll tell it to
you again.
I was only a guard at the time, sir, on the
London and Smash'em Line,
But I shan't forget the mishap to the eleven
sixty-nine.*

*'Twas a terrible foggy night, sir, and a day I
shan't forget.
The fog was a kind of Scotch mist, sir, and the
train it was somehow wet!
When all of a sudden I heard, sir, the sound of
a mighty crash.
I busied myself with the injured and helped
myself to their cash.*

*For the coaches were all of a heap, sir, though
why I cannot tell.
And the passengers lying around us were none
of 'em looking well.
They slept their last sleep on the sleepers, we
could hear the sleepers snore.
It's a sight I've never seen, sir, and shall never
see before.*

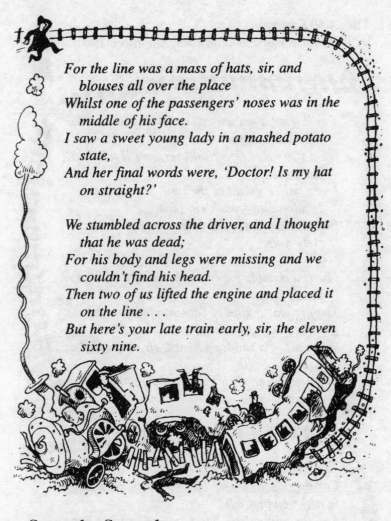

For the line was a mass of hats, sir, and
*   blouses all over the place*
Whilst one of the passengers' noses was in the
*   middle of his face.*
I saw a sweet young lady in a mashed potato
*   state,*
And her final words were, 'Doctor! Is my hat
*   on straight?'*

We stumbled across the driver, and I thought
*   that he was dead;*
For his body and legs were missing and we
*   couldn't find his head.*
Then two of us lifted the engine and placed it
*   on the line . . .*
But here's your late train early, sir, the eleven
*   sixty nine.*

Scott the Second

'Where there is a daring deed to be done in any part of the world, an Englishman should leap to the front to accomplish it.' Well, Captain Scott was that man.

In 1904 he went further south than any human had ever been before and came back safe. What a hero! The trouble was, he didn't know when to stop.

In 1910 he leapt off to the Antarctic a second time. He wanted to be the first man to reach the South Pole ... and came second.

• Scott and his team reached the South Pole on 18 January 1912, three weeks after the Norwegians led by Roald Amundsen (not to be confused with Roald Dahl who preferred writing books to crossing snowy wastes).

• Scott wrote, 'It is a terrible disappointment ... it will be a wearisome return.' It was worse than wearisome! It was *dead* wearisome. In fact they ended up wearisomely dead.

• Frostbite caused one of Scott's men to practically lose his nose. Scott was surprised that the man, 'shows signs of losing heart over it.' It seems 'losing heart' is just not *British* – 'losing nose' is all right.

• Scott became a hero even though he *failed*. In fact he probably became a hero *because* he failed. That's a very British thing to do. It would have been a bit embarrassing if he'd returned to Britain as a loser. If he had lived then his fellow Brits could hardly have patted him on the back and said, 'Better luck next time, old chap.' You can't have a second try at being 'first' when someone else has already done it, can you?

- If Scott was a hero then one of his men, Captain Oates, became a super-hero. He knew he was dying of frostbite so he walked out into the snow to die rather than depress his chums by dying in the tent. His famous last words were, 'I'm just going outside, and may be some time.' (In some versions of the story he said, 'I'm going out for a pee.' This is not so heroic or so British.)

- Captain Scott told the makers of Oxo that his men enjoyed Oxo and even sent a picture of them scoffing the stuff. The Oxo company quickly created a poster showing a polar bear enjoying some of Scott's Oxo … then someone told them that Polar Bears do not live at the South Pole – they live at the North Pole. The poster was quickly changed to show penguins.
- Before the expedition Captain Scott married his bride, Kathleen. Scott turned up for his wedding and brought with him a tall and handsome friend. 'Ohh!' Kathleen exclaimed, 'Do you think I could marry him instead?'

• The answer must have been 'No,' because they *did* marry and had a son, Peter. Sir Peter Scott grew to become a famous wildlife expert. One of the investigations he took part in was the search for the Loch Ness Monster. He even came up with a scientific name for it: *Nessiteras Rhombopteryx*. The support of such a famous man meant a lot of people began to take Nessie seriously … until someone worked out that the letters of *Nessiteras Rhombopteryx* could be rearranged to spell *Monster hoax by Sir Peter S!*

Wild women

The women who were fighting to get the vote faced a pretty tough time. Policemen were quite happy to beat and kick them as they carted them off to prison. When the women refused to eat in prison, the prison doctors had their own nasty methods of keeping the women alive.

Lady Constance Lytton disguised herself as a working woman and called herself Jane Warton when she was arrested. The 21-year-old Lady Constance didn't eat for four days. She describes what happened next …

> *The senior medical officer said, 'That is too long a time without food. I shall have to feed you at once,' but he went out and nothing happened until about six o'clock in the evening when he returned with five women warders and the feeding apparatus. He asked me to take food. I told him it was absolutely out of the question.*
>
> *He did not examine my heart or feel my pulse to see if I was fit to take the treatment. I offered no resistance, but lay down voluntarily on the plank bed. Two of the wardresses took hold of my arms, one held my head and one my feet. One wardress helped pour the food. The doctor leant on my knees as he stooped over my chest to get at my mouth. I shut my mouth and clenched my teeth.*

17

The doctor offered me the choice of a wooden gag or a steel gag. He explained that the steel gag would hurt and the wooden gag would not. He urged me not to force him to use the steel gag. But I did not speak or even open my mouth. After playing about for a moment or two with the wooden one he finally felt he had to use the steel. He seemed annoyed at my resistance and he broke into a temper as he plied my teeth with the steel instrument. He found that on either side at the back I had false teeth mounted on a bridge that I could not take out. The wardress asked if I had any false teeth, if so they must be taken out. I made no answer. He dug the instrument down on my false tooth, it pressed fearfully on the gum. He said if I resisted so much with my teeth he would have to feed me through the nose.

The pain of it was intense and at last I must have given way for he got the gag between my teeth. Then he proceeded to turn it more than necessary until my jaws were fastened wide apart, far more than they would naturally go. Then he put a tube down my throat which seemed much too wide and about four feet in length. The irritation of the tube was excessive. I choked the moment it touched my throat until I got it down.

Then the food was poured in quickly. It made me sick a few seconds after it was down and the action of the sickness made my body and legs double up, but the wardresses instantly pressed back my head and the doctor leant on my knees.

The horror of it was more than I can describe. I was sick over the doctor and the wardresses and it seemed a long time before they took the tube out. When the doctor had gone I lay quite helpless.

And you think Lady Constance had a rough time? One woman was force-fed 232 times!

The government came up with a new trick in 1913 – the Temporary Discharge for Ill-health Act. As soon as a suffragette became unwell from a hunger strike she was sent home. When she started eating at home and recovered the police arrested her and locked her up again. This cruel little 'game' was nicknamed the 'Cat and Mouse Act'.

   Of course, if starving yourself doesn't work then you can always try a bit of sarcasm. This poem was published by the Artists' Suffrage League …

Convicts and women, kindly note,
Are not allowed to have the vote;
The difference between the two
I will now indicate to you.
When once the harmful man of crime,
In Wormwood Scrubs has done his time,
He at the poll may have his say,
The harmless woman never may.

Then, in 1914, World War I started. Men went to France to fight and women took their places in the factories.

Women 'wore the trousers' for the first time. As a word-mangling song of the time advised women farm-workers ...

> *Dainty skirts and delicate blouses*
> *Aren't much use for pigs and cowses.*

OH, I SAY!

Women proved to be so capable that even men appreciated them. During the war men finally gave the vote to women – if they were over 30. There was a bit of a struggle before women over 21 could vote, giving them the same rights as men.

The Nineteen-tens

Sometimes an event happens that is so great the world is never the same again after it. In the twentieth century one of the greatest of those events is World War I – fought against Germany from 1914 till 1918. Everyone is in it together. Upper classes and lower classes, women as well as men. This 'mixing' has never happened before and it will change the way the classes look at each other.

The writer George Orwell sums it up, 'In 1910 every human being could be "placed" in an instant by his clothes, manners and accent. After 1918 there began to appear people with no clear social class.'

Timeline – 1910s

1910 London Council grants 87 licences for 'Electric Theatres' to open this year. An Electric Theatre is not a shocking entertainment – it's a *cinema*. (There are now 775 in the country.) They're very popular even though shows last just 15 minutes. The first Juvenile Courts (for children) are held in London. Kids' crimes include playing football in the street, gambling, throwing fireworks, insulting behaviour and (goodness knows why) 'shouting "Celery!"'.

1911 Suffragettes are locked in prison for acts of violence. They get their own back by refusing to eat food – hunger strikes. 2,100,000 women are servants and most earn about £15 a year. Men-servants, of

21

course, are paid three times as much. The Coal Mines Act insists on a 48-hour week and two weeks' holiday each year ... for the pit ponies!

1912 *Titanic* ship launched. They say it's *unsinkable*. Then ... the *unthinkable*. It sinks! 700 women, children and millionaires are first to the lifeboats but 1500 die a chilly death. So does Scott of the Antarctic. Meanwhile a man plans a sort of 'lifeboat' for those dangerous aeroplane things. Austrian Franz Reichelt invents a *parachute*. 'I am confident of success!' he announces before he jumps off the top of the Eiffel Tower. The parachute fails. Franz is scraped off the pavement. He'd have been better advised to try jumping off the *Titanic*.

1913 Those suffragette women make trouble again. One tries to stop the king's horse as it races in the Derby. Suffragette suffers death. Other suffragettes attack Prime Minister Asquith, bomb government minister David Lloyd George's home in Surrey, set fire to letters in pillar-boxes and even set fire to a railway station. (Maybe a suffragette thought they said *male-*way station.) And one quite poor woman is arrested simply for wearing a *split skirt* in Richmond Park! No wonder the women are revolting.

1914 George Bernard Shaw's play shocks London. A character says the word 'bloody'! A lot of people are saying that over the next four years as the Great War with Germany starts. Very bloody. A newspaper reported, 'Cheer after cheer from the crowds greeted the news that the Mother Country (Britain) had declared war against Germany.' Four 'bloody' years later they will be cheering that it's all over. Meanwhile a new law says you can only be whipped *once* for any one crime. (What a kind government.)

1915 Those troublesome women work in the factories, making ammunition for soldiers to shoot at the Germans. Production more than doubles. The Germans sink The *Lusitania* ship sailing from America – women, children and friends of US President Woodrow Wilson are killed. No one will be safe in this war. A vicar complains that the working classes spend too much time and money at cinemas – 'Cinemas are probably a more serious menace to the nation than even drink!' What would he have said about the television?

1916 Men 'conscripted' (forced) to fight for Britain. The army is getting short of men and no wonder. At the Battle of the Somme 19,000 are

dead after one day and after four months 420,000 men have been wounded, captured or killed. They gain two miles – that's a cost of about two men for every centimetre. **1917** Women in the factories earn the grudging gratitude of men, who give them the vote. USA enters the war (on the British side) while the Russians have a revolution and massacre their royal family. This makes the British royal family a bit nervous. Poor Brits have to eat 'War bread' made from very poor flour – it's a delicious shade of grey! British General Haig has learned nothing from the Somme disaster of last year. He sends still more troops to a muddy death in Flanders while saying, 'The enemy will collapse at any moment.' (How wrong can one man be?)

1918 World War I ends – four years and 767,000 dead Britons after it started. Britain and her allies win the war. British women give men their jobs back. British children win the honour of staying at school till they're 14. (Lucky kids!) Teachers have their wages doubled – luckier teachers!

1919 Just when you thought it was a safe world to live in ... Spanish 'flu strikes. The war killed 8.5 million around the world. Spanish 'flu kills 20 million in just two

years! And a new sweet is invented to celebrate peace – the Jelly Baby. A bit odd, this – the message seems to be, 'Think peaceful thoughts as you chew off a baby's head.' But the men had other things to worry about after the war …

Moaning men

World War I cost millions of lives. The surviving men came home and expected to be treated like heroes. They weren't. They weren't even sure of getting a job after four years of fighting for their country.

Many were bitter. They felt they'd been let down. This bitter mood is shown in the sort of recital they listened to in the Music Halls as entertainment. When H. M. Burnaby recited this poem in 1922 there must have been a lot of men in the audience who were nodding in agreement and muttering, 'That's just what happened to me ...'

Jimmy Johnson

*He was Mr Jimmy Johnson and he earned a weekly
    wage,*
And his life was as eventful as a squirrel in a cage.
*He possessed a wife and kiddies, living somewhere
    Brixton way,*
*And he drew his humble pittance, weekly, every
    Saturday.*
*And that was why he added rows of figures nice and
    neat,*
He was Mr Jimmy Johnson – life was sweet.

*Then somewhere a bugle sounded and he kissed his
    pen goodbye.*
*His stool he kicked from under him – no time to
    wonder why,*
*He embraced his wife and kiddies, and he told them
    not to pine.*

26

He was Private Jimmy Johnson, number 12129.
He didn't quite appreciate the stuff he'd got to eat,
But he was Private Johnson – life was sweet.

Now he's Mr Jimmy Johnson, and he's got an empty
  sleeve,
And he's smiling very bravely and it's so hard to
  believe
He's forgotten by the stay-at-homes – who not so long
  ago,
Said they didn't want to lose him, but they thought he
  ought to go.
You can see them all around you, some sell matches in
  the street,
There are many Jimmy Johnsons – is life sweet?

A soldier described his search for work in 1919 …

I walked around and eventually sat on a park bench. I must have dozed off because it was dark when I woke up. I decided to stay there until morning. I woke as the sun was rising and what a sight met my eyes. All the benches were full of old soldiers in all sorts of old clothes – mostly khaki – and others were lying on steps; some were wrapped in newspapers. These were the men who had fought in the trenches, now unwanted and left to starve, all huddled together.

This was in a country where Prime Minister Lloyd George promised that at the end of the war the men would come back to 'a land fit for heroes to live in.' Some land, some life.

The barmy Belgian battler

Britain is famous for its brave fighters. Men like Lord Nelson who lost an eye and an arm yet kept battling against the French in the Napoleonic Wars.

In World War I there were equally brave men. But the wackiest, most eccentric British soldier wasn't British. He was a Belgian who chose to fight for Britain. His name was Adrian Carton de Wiart …

1899

War broke out in South Africa so I joined the British Army—for a bit of adventure. Lied about my age and said I was British. If the British had turned me down I'd have joined the other side! I called myself Trooper Carton. When I was wounded they found out my real name. Dad was furious since I was only 19. Finally managed to persuade him to let me stay.

1914

More than ten years of Peace. God! I've been so bored. Now some Mad Mullah chap is making trouble in British Somaliland and I was delighted to be sent to sort him out.

A MULLAH → MAD → FURIOUS

Of course, I was furious when I heard there was a bigger and better war starting in Europe! Still, I led the attack against the Mad Mullah's fort carrying a broken polo stick. Chaps thought I was odd but I explained, "I refuse ⟶

to carry weapons in case I lose my temper and shoot my own men." That shut them up. I was just about to capture the fort when some blighter popped up with a gun and shot me in the eye!

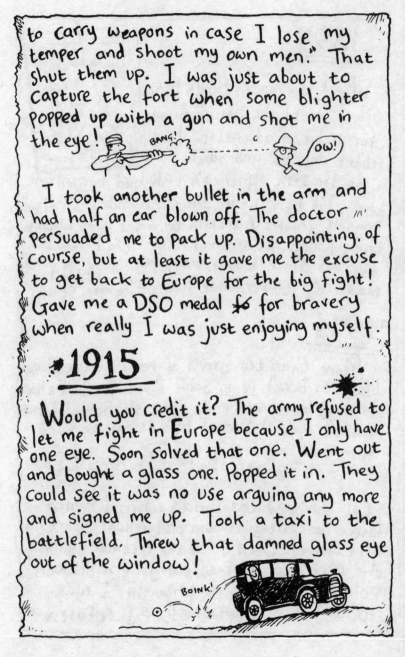

I took another bullet in the arm and had half an ear blown off. The doctor persuaded me to pack up. Disappointing, of course, but at least it gave me the excuse to get back to Europe for the big fight! Gave me a DSO medal £6 for bravery when really I was just enjoying myself.

1915

Would you credit it? The army refused to let me fight in Europe because I only have one eye. Soon solved that one. Went out and bought a glass one. Popped it in. They could see it was no use arguing any more and signed me up. Took a taxi to the battlefield. Threw that damned glass eye out of the window!

BOINK!

1916

Now they want to give me the Victoria Cross for leading my men into battle. Didn't actually shoot anyone myself since I was carrying a walking stick. Lost the damned thing when my hand was blown off in the attack – all but a couple of fingers, that is. The doctors refused to cut the remains off so I pulled them off. Threw them away too.

1919

Peace again. Rather tiresome so I'm off to fight in Poland. They really know how to have a decent war. They've got five going at once. Had a little difference of opinion with the British Army and resigned. Never mind. I like the Polish people better.

1940

Another nice big war. I'm only 60 so there are a few battles left in me yet. The British War Office sent for me. I had a feeling it might be to help out with Norway, especially since I've never been there and know nothing about it – and I was right. The Germans had just invaded and I joined the French in a secret commando force. The Germans had aircraft on patrol. Would you believe it? The crazy French started firing at the planes and gave our position away! The Germans replied with bombs. They sank a couple of our warships just off the coast. Pity I wasn't on board at the time. I've never been sunk—missed an interesting experience. Still, I escaped with my life as usual.

1944

Interesting few years. Set off for Yugoslavia in 1941. Unfortunately we crashed in North Africa and the Italians locked me up in one of their castles. Spent the next two years trying to escape. Managed eight days on the run once before I was recaptured.

TEASPOON FOR DIGGING ESCAPE TUNNELS

CUNNING DISGUISE

Then what did the Italians do? Took me to Rome, fitted me up with the best uniform money could buy and packed me back to England. They sent me with secret messages asking to make peace— secret because they didn't want their old German allies to know! Crazier than the French if you ask me. Still, they got the peace they wanted. There's only one thing I can't understand. Why would anyone want peace when war is so exciting?

Adrian Carton de Wiart was bored by peace in Europe in 1945 so British leader Winston Churchill sent him off to China where there was still fighting going on. De Wiart's last great mission was to deliver much needed gifts to the Chinese … cases of whisky! Of course, with Adrian Carton de Wiart on board, the plane *had* to crash – and of course, with Adrian Carton de Wiart on board not a drop of the precious whisky was lost!

Adrian was a Belgian who fitted in well with the quaint British idea of an eccentric. The Americans, on the other hand, did not see war as a sport. It was a matter of life or death. General Patton of the USA created America's first tank troop in World War I. He liked to give new recruits a pep-talk to stir them up. He would say, 'War is a killing business. You've got to spill their blood or they'll spill yours. Rip them up the belly or shoot them in the guts.'

Adrian Carton de Wiart went into battle with a polo stick – George Patton designed a special sword with extra-deep grooves on the side for the blood. It's strange to think that two men with such different opinions were on the same side in two wars!

Cheating Charlie

In 1915 the British Army was having a terrible time in the war. They were bogged down in mud in France and dying in the dust of the Dardanelles in Turkey.

There was just one bright spot for the British soldier ... the Camp Kinema where he could watch the silent films. And in 1915 a brilliant new film comedian appeared to make the soldiers laugh their lice-infested socks off. Charlie Chaplin.

Of course Charlie Chaplin was *British*. Were the British people proud of the clever tramp making it big in Hollywood? Were they? Er ... well ... to tell the truth not *everyone* was! The press reported with disgust that he should have been in uniform, fighting for his country and having his funny little bowler hat shredded by shrapnel.

The ordinary soldiers weren't so worried. (Why would they want another clown as a soldier in France when they had the British generals?) The soldiers just shrugged, took Charlie Chaplin's song and changed the words. As they marched along they sang ...

Oh the moon shines bright on Charlie Chaplin
His shoes are cracking, for want of blacking.
And his little baggy trousers they'll need mending
Before we send him
To the Dardanelles.

Charlie Chaplin made a film called *Soldier Arms* that made fun of the Germans. After that he was forgiven for not fighting.

The Sackville sob story

Lady Victoria-Josepha Sackville-West had money problems. She had a large house called Knole to keep and very little money. If her husband died then there would be huge taxes to pay – death duties. It was important that Lord Sackville should be kept alive as long as possible. Then disaster! World War I came along and he had to go to fight for his country. His death would spell calamity for Lady Victoria … and it wouldn't do much for Lord Sackville either.

That's when she had a brain-wave. She decided to write a letter of appeal to her dear friend, Lord Kitchener, the commander-in-chief of the British forces. Victoria-Josepha asked the general to give her hubby a safe job. She followed this with another letter of complaint. The letter is a window into the world of the upper-class Brits in the 1910s …

Dear Lord K.
   I think that perhaps you do not realise that we employ five carpenters and four painters and two footmen and you are taking them all away from us! I do not complain about the footmen – although I never thought I would see parlourmaids at Knole House. Dear Lord K, I am sure you will
P.T.O

sympathise with me when I say that parlourmaids are so middle-class, not at all what you and me are used to. But, as I said, that is not what I complain about; I know that we must set an example. You are at the War Office and must neglect your own dear Broome House, which I know you love so much. I think you love it as much as I love Knole. And, of course, you must love it even more because the world says you never loved any woman – is that true? I shall ask you next time I come to luncheon with you. But talking about luncheon reminds me of parlourmaids and I said that I would not complain about them (because I am patriotic after all) but I _do_ complain about the way you take our footmen from us.

Victoria~Josepha

Luckily for Lord Kitchener he didn't have to suffer being nagged by her ladyship at 'luncheon' – he was killed in 1916 when his ship hit a mine and sank.

Silly Sitwell
Sir George Sitwell had similar problems coping with the idea of war. World War I was fought largely in muddy trenches with the enemies trying to blast each other to pieces with shells. Sir George wrote to advise his son, Osbert ...

Dear Osbert

Directly you hear the first shell retire to the cellar and remain there until all firing has ceased. Even then, a bombardment is a strain upon the nervous system. The best remedy for that is to keep warm and have plenty of plain, nourishing food at regular intervals. And, of course. plenty of rest. I find a nap in the afternoon most helpful and I advise you to try it whenever possible.

love Dad.

Sir George hadn't a *clue* what war at the front line was really like. The real tragedy was that generals like Brit Commander Haig didn't have a clue either! It's a pity George and the generals couldn't have read a poem that a front-line Sergeant Major wrote …

You stand in a trench of vile stinking mud
And the bitter cold wind freezes your blood
Then the guns open up and the flames light the sky
And, as you watch, rats go scuttling by.

The men in the dugouts are quiet for a time
Trying to sleep midst the stench and the slime.
The moon is just showing from over the Hill
And the dead on the wire hang silent and still.

A sniper's bullet wings close to your head
As you wistfully think of a comfortable bed.
But now a dirty blanket has to suffice
And more often than not it is crawling with lice.

Haig and his mob keep well in the rear,
Living in luxury, safe in old St Omer,
Flashing red tabs, brass and ribbons galore,
What the Hell do they know about fighting a War?

After World War I it was going to be harder for the selfish Sackville or the sackless Sitwell to ignore the cruelty of the real world. After World War I the world could never be the same again. Ever.

The Trendy Twenties

One of the great changes after World War I is that there are fewer families with servants. After the gloomy war years the young rich people are having a wild time and will name the age the Roaring Twenties. When the poor workers go on strike in 1926, rich people think it's fun to drive buses and fire engines to keep the country going. They dance the energetic Charleston in short dresses (the women, not the men) while the poor get poorer.

Timeline – 1920s

1920 A million men have lost their jobs and that will rise to two million in the next six months. After the war Prime Minister Lloyd George had promised 'to make Britain a fit country for heroes to live in.' The men now feel a bit cheated. Even the lucky ones in work have their wages cut.

1921 Convicts in prisons no longer have their hair cropped and large arrows printed on their uniforms … artists who draw children's comics continue to give convicts arrows for the next 90 years! And criminals have a new enemy … Agatha Christie invents the brilliant Hercule Poirot to detect their crimes.

1922 British adventurers back on the trail. This time the Earl of Caernarvon's expedition digs up Tutankhamun's mummy (but not his daddy). The government is short of money so it cuts teachers' wages!

39

1923 In the past if a woman committed a crime then her husband was responsible. Under a new law the woman is responsible for her own crimes.

1924 'The subjection of women has certainly passed forever,' the *Daily Mail* declares. (Ho! Ho!) Then it warns … 'It seems almost as if the subjection of men might be beginning.' (This was, of course, written by a man.)

1925 Great British invention – white lines down the middle of the road. They don't help with a new British problem – traffic jams. Cars, taxis and buses in London's Strand are unable to move for two hours. Skegness sees the introduction of something that could solve all London's problems … the first *dodgem cars* in Britain!

1926 Even greater British invention – television. John Logie Baird demonstrates his 'pictures by radio' in London. Meanwhile there is a 'General Strike' of miners, transport workers and many others. The government appoints 140,000 special policemen to sort the strikers out. The special police don't have enough truncheons to go round so they send a lorry-load of chair legs. Ouch!

1927 Brit hero Major Henry

Seagrave beats world land speed record at over 200 m.p.h. But he does this in America where there are no policemen with stopwatches to arrest him. He also avoids the new Brit invention – electric traffic lights. (Victorian gas ones had been known to blow up!) Meanwhile American hero Charles Lindberg is the first man to fly across the Atlantic Ocean alone.

1928 Britain holds another world record – an average of 1.5 kg of tobacco per year smoked by every Brit man and woman (and child). The craziest crazes of the time include jumping around on pogo sticks and racing on wooden rocking-horses. Women of 21 get the vote. On the same day that law is passed the great suffragette Emmeline Pankhurst is buried.

1929 A young woman stabs a man and is blackmailed! That's the plot of the first British talking picture, directed by Alfred Hitchcock. A cure for wrinkles is suggested – radioactive mud spread over the face!

Sweet Suzie
Daring dresses and heroic haircuts

Women had been given the vote in 1917. Now they found the strength to challenge men and the older generation about how they dressed. They rebelled against stuffy old long skirts and instead wore ones that showed their legs, and dresses that flattened their chests.

Then women grew really daring as they cut their hair short in a 'bob' and they showed the world ... their ears! An even shorter haircut was called a 'shingle' and they became really boyish with an 'Eton' cut.

Men, of course, couldn't stop these women's fashions. All they could do was try to poke fun at them. They sang this tongue-twisting song in 1924. Can you recite it in under 15 seconds? Suzie Simpson supposedly sang ...

'Shall I have it bobbed or shingled?
Shall I have it shingled or bobbed?'
Sister Cissie says, 'Oh have it shorn short, Sue,
Shingled, shorn and shaven like the swell set do.'
'Shall I have it shingled shorter?'
Said Sue as she sighed and sobbed;
'Sister Cissie says she'd sooner see it short and
*   shingled,*
But both my brothers, Bert and Bobbie, say it's better
*   bobbed!'*

Women who were married to unemployed men didn't have Suzie's problem, of course. They couldn't even afford reasonable clothes never mind luxuries like a haircut. They wore shapeless skirts and aprons made of sacking.

It's smart to smoke … NOT!
Many women copied the men's habit of smoking cigarettes. Advertising persuaded them it was really much healthier than eating!

THE **THREAT** OF LOSING A TRIM SLENDER FIGURE!

HOW TO AVOID THAT FUTURE SHADOW

Ask your doctor! Overweight is harmful and destroys the trim, slender figure of fashion. And overweight is generally caused by eating between meals. That's the time to smoke **KENSITAS** instead. Your desire will be pleasantly forgotten in the mellow satisfaction of the appetising aroma of **KENSITAS**

This 'fat is bad' message has led to years of misery for some women as they diet – the 'smoking is good for you' message led to more misery as they died.

Cane pain

Teachers in the Twenties could slap the back of your legs or rap your knuckles with a ruler. But the greatest punishment was 'the cane'. This was usually a thin bamboo rod, nice and springy with a hiss like a bullet as it swished through the air. You'd be caned across the backside or across the hand – the teacher would probably cane the hand you *didn't* write with so you could get on with your work straight away.

A crack on the ear or the back of the head was quite normal but caning was taken more seriously. Firstly, it was usually carried out in front of the whole class, or even the whole school, so everyone could see what happened to wicked children. Then the punishment was written down in a punishment book. As a result we know the sort of 'crimes' that children committed in the Twenties.

Boys tried to look on the cane as a challenge. They couldn't show that it hurt them in the slightest ... and boys daren't ever cry. Girls often saw the cane as a more embarrassing thing. There are many cases of girls screaming and sobbing when they were taken to the front of the class to be caned – in many cases the teacher got another teacher to hold her still so she could be beaten.

Which of the following were punished with the cane in a Birmingham girls' school?

Answer: All of them. And these are the 'good old days' that grandparents talk about! It wasn't unusual for a pupil's finger to be broken or for a teacher to break a cane over a pupil's hand.

Did you know…?
On 12 September 1911, London schoolboys went on strike! They wanted an extra half day's holiday and they wanted the cane banned. They didn't get the extra holiday … and, of course, when they returned to school they were punished for walking out. They were caned!

The Bear Game

In the Twenties someone invented the Bear Game. It can be played by almost anyone, it costs nothing … and it is pointless, idiotic and offensive. (Just the sort of game you like playing.)

How to play
1 You need two or more to play.
2 Quite simply you walk along a street (or through a shopping centre or anywhere that crowds gather). The first person to spot a beard shouts, 'Bear!' and gets a point. And the first to get 20 points is the winner.
3 Extra points can be given for certain beards – a white beard and a cry of 'Polar Bear!' or a beard that touches the chest and a cry of 'Grizzly Bear!' could earn two points each.

Did you know…?
This incredibly stupid game led to a change in fashions! Men were so embarrassed at being shouted at in the street that they began to shave off their beards. By 1924 beards were so scarce on men (and even rarer on women) that the game was abandoned.

One person who refused to give up his beard was King George V. But he had some peculiar fashions anyway. In the 1910s, when every upper class man was wearing a top hat, the king wore a soft felt hat known as a 'homburg'. The upper classes copied him. He also wore his trouser creases at the *sides* of his trousers and not at the front and back. This fashion did *not* catch on!

Bright young things

Some of the upper classes of the Twenties were *jealous* of the lower classes. 'It is all very well for the working man who has his job and his struggle for existence,' a poet called Eliot moaned. 'What remains for the modern man?' he asked. Mr Eliot never offered to swap places with a coal-miner or a steel-worker, you understand!

So, what could these people do to enjoy a good 'struggle'? The answer? Crazes. Doing entertaining things – or just plain *silly* things.

47

Clubs

The Universities at Oxford and Cambridge had two rival groups. The ones who went there to have a good time (the 'Hearties') and those who went there to study (the 'Swots'). Of course, just as at most schools, the Hearties made fun of the Swots. But, unlike most schools, the Swots fought back – one drew a sword and cut off the thumb of a Hearty who was tormenting him.

The Hearties formed silly clubs:

• 'The Hide and Seek Club' played hide-and-seek in and out of the houses of the rich people of Oxford.

• 'The University Pavement Club' decided not to be part of the hustle and bustle of Twenties life. They spent an hour every Saturday sitting on the pavement of the main street and playing tiddlywinks, noughts and crosses, card games or knitting.

- 'The Oxford Railway Club' travelled on an express train late at night, got off and travelled back on the next express. They were able to have dinner on the first train and make speeches on the way back.

- Climbing clubs didn't want the bother of going to the mountains, so they climbed over the college buildings. These ancient buildings were often damaged by the climbers but these Bright Young Things weren't too worried about that. They proved their bravery each time by placing a chamber pot over a chimney. The police shot it down with a rifle. But if it was a metal pot the police had to climb up with scaffolding to get it down. This wasted more valuable police time and money. The Bright Young Things weren't too worried about that either – after all, it wasn't their money.

Parties

Treasure hunts through the late-night streets of London were popular. So were silly parties: fancy-dress parties, swimming parties, Mozart parties (with Mozart-age costumes and dances) and parties where people went dressed as their own ancestors. A simple and popular party of the

Twenties was to dress up as children and spend the whole evening behaving like children. (You may find this difficult but teachers are very good at this sort of performance. Ask one to give you a demonstration.)

And parties wouldn't be the same without a good dance. Some people today remember the Black Bottom, the Charleston and the Shimmy. Sadly we've forgotten …
• the Vampire
• the Elfreda
• the Twinkle
• the Jog Trot
• the Camel Walk (one hump or two, I wonder?)

Pogo sticks
A pogo stick (if you don't know) is a stick with a cross piece that you put your feet on. The bottom is sprung so you can bounce along (or fall flat on your face, if you prefer). Today it's a children's toy but in the 1920s the Bright Young Things

raced on them down the streets of London. Children who could afford them could join the *Daily News*'s Japhet Club with a cartoon, pogo-jumping hero called Japhet.

In competitions a record was held by a Bristol boy who managed 1600 hops in 15 minutes and covered a third of a mile in eight minutes. This craze may seem silly to us, but what would the Bright Young Things have said about the 1990s craze for bungee jumping?

Put and take

In 1922 everyone was playing this game. Everywhere! In pubs and schools and on trains. Try it for yourself and see if you can work out why it was so popular.

You need a piece of card with six sides and about 4cm in width. Each side has a different instruction as follows: Put one; Put two; Put three; Take one: Take two; Take all. A matchstick is pushed through the centre of the card to make a spinner.

Use matchsticks as counters. Each player starts with (say) 20 matches. Before each spin everyone puts a match onto the table. Players spin the spinner in turn and each one follows the instruction that appears on the top side. So, for example, if the instruction says, 'Take one', the player takes one of the matches from another player. Players drop out when they have lost all their matches. The winner is the one to end up with all the matches.

Tasteless toe-warmers

Shoemakers of the 1920s were not great at conserving wildlife. In fact they would use anything to make shoes – so long as the public wanted to buy them. Which of the following materials were used to make shoes?

Hits and misses

Remember Sir Claude Champion de Crespigny, 'Where there is a daring deed to be done in any part of the world, an Englishman should leap to the front to accomplish it'? The 1900s had been a bad time for Brit 'leapers' – the Americans had reached the North Pole first and the Norwegians had reached the South Pole.

The Twenties was a fine decade for Brit heroes to leap to the front. But the person at the front is often the first to slip on the banana skin. Brave Brits leapt and achieved glorious success … or miserable failure.

Here are some famous attempts. What happened next…?

1 Up the pole

After Scott's heroic but disasterous attempt to reach the South Pole in 1912, Sir Ernest Shackleton set off in 1921 for another chilly picnic. His job was to map it and claim the South Pole for Britain. Before he set off his ship, *The Quest*, was anchored in the River Thames and visitors flocked to see it. But there was an added attraction.

There was a competition to win a spare place on the expedition for the handiest, toughest Boy Scout who applied. (Boy Scouts are good with compasses and maps. Scott didn't take a Boy Scout. That could have been Scott's big mistake.)

A Scottish boy called Marr won this great competition, beating thousands of other idiots who wanted to sample the delights of frostbite, penguin–attack and sea-sickness. Shackleton reached the shores of Antarctica. What happened next…?

2 In a flap

Flying across the Atlantic Ocean was a great Brit dream. In 1919 Major Wood and Captain Wyllie tried to fly from Britain to America. That is east to west. The winds generally blow from west to east, so they were doing it the hard way. Just to make sure God would give them a hand, their aeroplane was blessed by a priest and they set off. They came down in the Irish Sea. (Look at a map to see how far they got. Not far. Rather like tripping over the starting blocks in a 100-metre sprint. God must have been busy elsewhere that day.)

So, star test-pilot Harry Hawker and chum Commander Kenneth Mackenzie-Grieve decided to try flying west to east – much more sensible. They had huge amounts of publicity whipped up by their sponsors, the *Daily Mail*. Their plane had a built-in boat – incredibly sensible, for a Brit! What happened next…?

3 Perils for pilots
Captain Alcock and Lieutenant Brown of the Royal Air Force set off a month after Harry Hawker. They used a Vickers Vimy bomber. (Being even more sensible than Harry Hawker they left their bombs behind. Being even more daring they didn't have a boat attached to their plane.) Being true Brit heroes they didn't bother with lots of those newspaper chappies giving them publicity. This was not a newspaper stunt – this was a serious adventure. What happened next…?

4 Awesome airships
General Maitland was in charge of a huge hydrogen-filled airship. This gallant airman and his crew crossed the Atlantic and became the first men to reach America from Britain by air. By the time they reached New York there was just an hour's petrol left for the engines. Phew, that was a close-run thing, chaps!

Then – more drama! A stowaway was found in the airship gas-bags! (After all the storms and the bumpy ride he must have wished he hadn't bothered!)

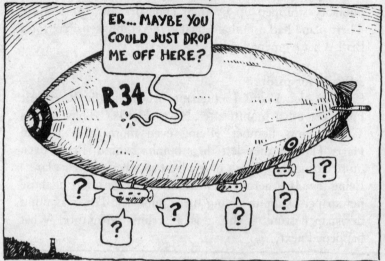

Then, still greater drama!!! General Maitland, floating over New York, had a problem. The people on the ground had never had to handle one of these airship things before. How could the men on the ground be taught how to bring the great balloon down safely? Major Pritchard stepped forward. 'I have an idea, sir!' What happened next...?

5 Around the world in 80 bits

Australians are different from Brits. They do things the *really* hard way. Two Australians, M'Intosh and Parer, decided to fly home from Britain. They bought an old plane from World War I for a few pounds – and that was expensive because almost everything about it was faulty! They then set off and ...

- caught fire over France – then dived steeply to blow out the fire
- had engine problems and were forced to land in the central Arabian desert. M'Intosh held tribesmen off with

hand-grenades and a pistol while Parer repaired the engine. They took off just in time

- made a forced landing in the Irawaddy jungle in India but took off again only to crash again and wreck the undercarriage, the radiator and the compass. They fixed the plane in the jungle after six weeks and took off again
- after two more crashes reached the shark-infested Timor Sea and became lost when their instruments proved faulty

- crashed at Culcairn, almost home, and stepped out of their plane, alive
- were given medals by the Australian Prime Minister

- the bits of their plane were put together one last time and placed in Sydney museum. Parer ran an airline. As for the indestructible M'Intosh, what happened next…?

Answers: **1** Shackleton caught the 'flu and died. The rest of the expedition didn't fancy making the trip without him so they pottered around the edge of the Antarctic, then came home. **2** After 14 hours' flying they came down in the Atlantic and were rescued by a Danish steam ship. There was no wireless on the ship so Britain waited anxiously, desperate for news when they didn't land in Ireland. Then the newspapers proclaimed, 'HAWKER SAFE'. ('Kenneth Mackenzie-Grieve Safe' wouldn't have fitted on the front page.) They landed in Scotland, took a train south and were cheered like heroes at every station. They reached London to a welcome as great as if they had swum the Atlantic! Brits love a trier. **3** Alcock and Brown made it. They landed in Ireland after 1,880 miles and 16 hours. The nice green field they chose to land in turned out to be an Irish bog. Their plane began to sink in it as they scrambled to safety. What about the cheering crowds to celebrate this great occasion? Well, there were a few cows and a donkey and that was about it. Alcock and Brown's radio had packed up so no one knew where they were – they had to find the nearest phone and ask to be picked up. (Finding the nearest phone was more than Scott of the Antarctic managed.) The newspapers hadn't arranged the flight so the intrepid airmen didn't become the sort of heroes that huge-flop Hawker became! The King made them Sir Alcock and Brown, so that was all right. **4** Major Pritchard jumped out of the airship and landed safely. He used a parachute! (Bet you didn't think of that.) The R34 landed safely. Great sporting achievement but of little practical use. Ocean liners were safer and more comfortable than these big airbags. When the huge R101 airship crashed in 1929 and killed over 40 people the public said 'No thanks' to airship travel … even with a free parachute thrown in. **5** His luck ran out. He crashed in another plane – not such a lucky plane – and died.

Which of these conquering, questing men was the greatest hero? And which the greatest clown? Britain wanted to have the fastest humans on land, sea and air, but the effort cost lives. The cruellest death was probably that of Parry Thomas who broke the land-speed record on Pendine Sands in Carmathenshire, Wales. Trying to go faster still, the driving chain of his car snapped and wrapped itself around his neck. It was a quick death – 178 m.p.h. to be exact.

The Threadbare Thirties

The average family now has to live on £3 a week and the really poor live on bread, tea and potatoes. (Not all on the same plate, stupid!) People are encouraged to be healthy and take part in hiking, cycling and team sports. Just as well, really, because you have to pay a lot of money to visit a doctor. You can't afford to be ill! The comedian Groucho Marx called this decade the 'Threadbare Thirties'. For once he wasn't joking!

Timeline – 1930s

1930 Great British invention, the R101 airship, sets off on maiden voyage – the *Titanic* of the air. Filled with explosive gas (because that's cheaper) it crosses the Channel … and explodes. Forty-eight dead. (Back to the drawing board, chaps.) The famous British writer, D. H. Lawrence, dies. His girlfriend has his ashes tipped into a concrete mixer and used the concrete to build her new mantelpiece. The really bad news is there are two million unemployed and lots of hungry families in Britain.

1931 The government, worried by road accidents, starts a 'Safety First' campaign. Advice to pedestrians includes, 'Do not read newspapers as you cross the roads,' and, 'Do not drop parcels in the middle of busy streets.' Now you know.

1932 Record three million

60

unemployed now. This is the Great Depression. (*You'd* be depressed if you were starving.) Mars Bars are invented – but a Mars a day can't help you 'work, rest and play' when you have *no* work … and no *money* to buy one. Poor old teachers get a pay cut (again!) to help the government save money. (Heh! Heh!)

1933 Britain becomes a bit nervous when a Mr A. Hitler is made German Chancellor. (Rearrange the letters A. Hitler to make 'The liar' – is this a clue to the sort of man he is?) At the cinema, audiences see 'The Invisible Man' … or rather they *don't* see the Invisible Man. (If you see what I mean.) Sliced bread first sold in Britain. (Rearrange the letters to make 'Edible cards' – is this a clue to its taste?) People begin to report a strange creature in Loch Ness – and start a monster hunt that has gone on ever since.

1934 Mr Oswald Mosley in Britain thinks a dictator like Mr A. Hitler would be a jolly good thing for Britain. People can go to Mosley's meetings and agree – or disagree and get beaten up before being thrown out. Children are more interested in a new series of toys – Dinky cars. Meanwhile, big cars are not allowed to sound their horns after 11:30 p.m., so all–night hooting

61

is banned. (There are probably a lot of disappointed owls.)

1935 A steam train reaches 108 m.p.h. on the London-to-Newcastle line, British speedster Sir Malcolm Campbell reaches a land-speed record of 301 m.p.h. in the USA and British motorists now have a 30 m.p.h. speed limit in built-up areas. For £385 you can always buy a Jaguar car and drive at 90 m.p.h. – if you can find a good enough road.

1936 First BBC television broadcasts – if you can afford the £110 for a set. The unemployed can't. Two hundred unemployed men march from Jarrow in north-east England to London with a petition asking the government to help create jobs. After weeks of marching they reach London … and Prime Minister Baldwin refuses to meet them. They go home to houses without the new television sets – or even a loo. A guide to seasickness is published entitled 'Why bring that up?' George V dies, his son Edward VIII takes the crown, then gives it up to marry a divorced American woman (shock-horror) and the crown ends up on George VI's head. Three kings in one year!

1937 The first holiday camp is opened by Mr Billy Butlin at Skegness. The Chief Constable of

Bradford blames parents for wicked children. He says parents 'gamble on football pools, horses and dog racing which must have a harmful influence on the young'. (So, next time you're in trouble say, 'It's your fault, Mum, for buying a lottery ticket!') Police also suggest spankings and beatings – especially for boys. Worries about a war with Germany grow and Air-Raid Wardens are trained – just in case. There's a war started in Spain – the German airforce joins one side to practise its bombing! Rice pudding sold in cans for the first time. Do *not* throw this rice at weddings!

1938 Prime Minister Chamberlain signs an agreement with that friendly Mr Hitler chap in Germany. It says Britain and Germany will 'never go to war with one another again'. British MP Mr Winston Churchill thinks Mr Hitler is not only a nasty man but a liar. All kids are given gas masks – just in case Mr Churchill is right and Mr Chamberlain is wrong. The National Unemployed Workers Movement holds 'hunger strikes' in Britain. They stop traffic in London by lying down in the roads. The posters say, 'Work or Bread' – but the hunger strikers get neither.

1939 Mr 'Britain-and-Germany-

will-never-go-to-war-with-one-another-again' Chamberlain announces, 'This country is now at war with Germany.' There's a false air-raid alarm seconds after the announcement. British fighter-planes 'scramble' and take to the air. One airman shoots and kills another by mistake. That's just the start of six years of death and destruction.

The wonder of wireless

Have you ever listened to a radio broadcast at school? You probably never listened to one like this wartime children's programme ...

Put your books down and get your gas masks out. I want you to put them on and let's see if everyone can get it right this time. Wait a minute!

Remember, chin in – right in – first before you start, then pull the straps over your head. Now, don't rush – take your time. There you are, you see? You'll have to start all

Imagine that! Suffocating with a mask over your face while you struggle with your needles! Anyone with any sense would knit a very thick tea cosy and stick it over the radio. If you think school radio was bad you should have sampled school dinners. A Ministry of Food leaflet suggested lunches might include …

Big Brother on holiday

The organization of 'Mass Observers' was set up at the end of the 1930s to watch the British people at work and play and report on them. (You might like to try this harmless little hobby for yourself. Of course people get a bit nervous when you start 'observing' them and they might either report you to the police or punch you on your nosey bit.)

The Mass Observers went to Blackpool in the summer of 1937 to see the Brits on holiday. They picked a bad time.

Blackpool was full up. The Observers had to sleep on the beach and 'observe' seagulls all night! They reported that …
• nearly all of the men on holiday wore stiff starched collars and ties

• the sea-front was packed with rickety shops – mainly joke shops, fortune-tellers, cafés and amusement arcades

• souvenir shops were selling models of the Blackpool Tower and joke hats with 'Kiss me quick' written on them

• a pleasure beach where the big attraction was 'Noah's Ark' – a huge ship with life-sized models inside. (The door was not guarded by Noah, but by a mechanical policeman who bent at the knees!) Inside the Ark there were dark passageways and hands that grabbed you. Children enjoyed it – adults said they were terrified!

• there was a waxworks museum copied from Madame Tussaud's in London.

The fairground freak

Entertainments could be cruel in the 1930s but one of the saddest was the Rector of Stiffkey. This pathetic man had been thrown out of his job as a vicar and turned up in Blackpool in 1937 as a fairground freak. He decided to starve himself for a while – to 'fast'. He was put in a tent where he sat in a barrel and people paid to see him not eating! The police added to the excitement by arresting him on a charge of 'attempting suicide by starvation'. He was found innocent.

His next public appearance was at a London fair where he posed with a dead whale – today, that would be called 'Art'. Of course, the public became a little bit bored with this 'entertainment' so the next year he moved to the east-coast seaside town of Skegness. He decided to liven up his performance by entering a lion's cage. The lion, it seems, did not agree with this 'fasting' lark and quickly ate the poor Rector of Stiffkey.

Perhaps the Rector should have just said 'Kiss me quick' ... then left.

Lucky for some

Are you superstitious? Do you believe Friday 13th is an unlucky day? Brit hero, Henry Seagrave, wasn't worried about little things like that. He wanted to be the first human to do 100 m.p.h. on water. On Friday 13 June 1930 the conditions on Lake Windermere were perfect and his boat, *Miss England II*, was ready.

On the first run our Henry managed 96 m.p.h. He tried again. This time he did 101 m.p.h. But he needed *two* runs at over 100 miles an hour. He set off a third time.

Third time lucky? No.

Thirteen unlucky? Yes.

At top speed his propellers hit something in the water and snapped off. *Miss England II* shot up in the air, tumbled down and sank.

Seagrave was rescued but several of his ribs were smashed. He managed four words. Every one was agony. 'Did – we – do – it?'

He saw the rescuers nod ... then he died. Happy.

Happy families

The 'Depression' of the Thirties brought misery to millions. Yet some people tried to look on the bright side of the very worst times. In 1934 the BBC broadcast interviews with unemployed men and women. Mrs Pallas describes the most miserable existence. Would you be able to survive?

If only my husband had work. Just imagine what it would be like. On the whole he has worked one year out of twelve-and-a-half. His face was lovely when I married him, but now he's skin and bones.

He fell out of work four months after I married him so I've hardly known what a week's wage was. Through all the struggling I've still not lost my respectability. About four years ago I still managed to win a competition for the best-kept home. The bedclothes were all mended but at least they were clean. The originals you could hardly have known for the patches on.

My children wouldn't go to school with a hole in their trousers. My eldest boy has trousers on at the moment with six patches on them. I just tell him he'll be all the warmer, especially in winter. My husband helps me with the darning, I do the patching. I've just put the eighth patch on a shirt of his. I take the sleeves out of one and put them in another. Anything to keep going.

Then, when we've finished with the clothes, my husband puts them into making a mat. Many a time my husband has had to make cups for the children out of empty condensed milk tins. He solders handles on.

Our kettle's got about six patches on it. My husband made the patches from cocoa tins. My husband does all that sort of patching, all the cobbling and hair-cutting and spring-cleaning. I've always tried to keep my house looking nice. I feel as if I want to be the same as everybody else. It's the children I feel sorry for. That's what I fight for; not for myself.

My husband never spends any of his dole money on himself, still we can't manage. And we don't waste nothing. And there's no enjoyment comes out of our money – no pictures, no papers, no sports.

We're both of us always occupied in the home. I haven't had a holiday for thirteen years. My husband's never been to a football match. When people talk about the talking pictures I don't know what they mean. I've never been, I've no desire to go.

Now that eggs are cheap we use quite a lot. We very, very rarely get cheese. We all like it, but it's a bit of a luxury. When there are birthdays we have it. I can't manage more than one box of matches a week – that's all we ever use. Many a night we've sat in the dark – it's a gas light and maybe we haven't a penny for the slot or maybe we haven't a match. Rather than let people know, we sat in the dark.

I don't know what the boys'll do when they leave school. I think they ought to know what's happening in the world, but we can't afford a newspaper.

All the struggling is just for food. Still, we're happier than some, for in our house we're all in harmony, we all help. The kids wash the dishes and so on.

The only hope we've got is the hope to come. I've lived on hope for thirteen years.

Perhaps, after all, it's worse for the men. The women have their work and their home. I have no hope that my husband will ever work again.

Unhappy families

Not everyone coped with poverty and large families so well. This gruesome story happened in the Reporters' Room of a large London newspaper and it is supposed to be true …

This story may seem unlikely but then newspaper reporters don't seem so sensitive as the rest of us. Even in 1991 they were just as ruthless. There were riots on the streets of Meadow Well Estate in North Shields. The *Newcastle Journal* reporters were thinking of how many extra copies they'd sell when people rushed to read about it.

'We'd have sold hundreds in Meadow Well itself,' one journalist sighed. 'But the rioters burned down the newspaper shop.'

'What a nuisance!' groaned his fellow-reporters.

Awesome adverts

The Victorians had learned the power of advertising. Cigarette producers hooked millions of people on the habit through large advertising campaigns. Other manufacturers learned from this. One of the most successful was Pears' soap. Striking pictures with clever slogans covered the country. The most successful said, 'Good morning! Have you used Pears' Soap?'

In the 20th century, advertising 'grew up' and became cleverer and more powerful. One of the great adverts of the century was …

Message … Join the army, fight for your country and die 'gloriously' in freezing, rat-infested, mud-filled trenches.

But in 1939 World War II started and the posters were being aimed not at the soldiers but at the public, giving them encouragement …

This may be true but it is harder digging a garden with a sewing machine. German spies seeing this advert must have been puzzled.

Of course, many products were not made at all during the war – the factories were needed for war materials. But they were advertised anyway! The makers didn't want the public to forget their name.

One advert showed an elegant room with people eating a box of Caley's chocolates. 'What's wrong with this picture?' the caption asked. The answer was that you couldn't actually *buy* Caley's chocolates because of the war. This must have made chocoholics furious. In revenge they *did* forget Caley's chocolates after the war.

The most unfortunate advert of this kind was a 1939 one for Standard Fireworks which said, 'You can't have fireworks yet, but it may not be long now!' Soon after the advert appeared, Mr Hitler provided more 'fireworks' than anyone would ever want! But the advert didn't stop Standard Fireworks being used after the war.

Those things that you *could* buy were advertised as war-winners. Wolsey socks tried to persuade you that shorter socks saved material. They wanted to say 'Go in for shorter socks' – but that didn't rhyme so the advert became …

The government's hardest job was probably persuading people that the revolting dried eggs were just as good as fresh eggs. Firstly they *told* the public they were good and then they gave them recipes to choke on …

And a lot of people did 'swear' when they ate powdered egg!

The Fighting Forties

Bombs, bullets and blitzes for some people. Shortages of food, clothing, soap and almost everything else for most people. In fact people become more careful about the food they eat and, by the end of the war, the Brits are generally healthier than in the Thirties – unless they've been hit by a bomb, of course.

Timeline – 1940s

1940 Mr Winston 'Don't-trust-Hitler' Churchill is made Prime Minister. Mr Oswald 'Hitler's-a-nice-chap' Mosley is stuck in prison. The 'Battle of Britain' is fought between the German and British air forces. British cities suffer bombing – the Blitz. Food is rationed.

1941 Unmarried women can be called up to join the armed forces of Britain or directed to work in industry or on the land. The government refuses to let women have guns. They can repair aircraft and roads, catch rats, make bombs or dig in the fields … but they can't be let loose with a pistol. Clothes are now rationed. President Roosevelt brings the United States into the war against Japan, which is an ally of Germany. This cheers the blitzed Brits up. The US brings in lots of new tanks, planes and guns to fight with – and lots of new chewing-gum for the kids to stick to Teacher's chair.

1942 Nearly everything is in short supply or on ration because of the war. But ruthless people find ways to beat the rationing system. There are many cases, like the one of the butcher who sold 'stewing steak' to a restaurant – it turned out to be horsemeat. (He went to prison for six months.) Unscrupulous farmers are selling sick cattle to butchers. Your motto should be, 'Don't eat the sausages!' Women are wearing shorter skirts again – not because they are rebels (like the 1920s Bright Young Things) but because they just don't have enough material for long ones. And boys are stuck in short trousers till they're 12. Chilly kneecaps.

1943 The first 'Pop Star' is created in America. His name is Frank Sinatra. Meanwhile, clever Brit inventor (Barnes Wallis) invents a bomb that bounces! The bomb destroys three dams in Germany's Ruhr valley and they leak gallons of water. In British pubs they are selling gallons of water … except it is supposed to be beer. It is only half as strong as beer before the war – and you probably have to take your own glass to the pub.

1944 There are so many blood donations during World War II that there is some left over. Someone suggests that this spare

79

blood could be used to make black puddings and help with the food shortages. (The Government thinks seriously about this before finally rejecting the idea.) Married women can now become teachers.

1945 End of war with Germany. Atom bomb drops on Japan and that ends World War II. British people thank Mr Churchill by throwing his party out of power.

1946 War over but not the suffering. World food shortage, queues for bread, and rations for almost everything else. America orders that swimming costumes should use ten per cent less material – no problem! Cut out the bit in the middle … and what have they got? A bikini! (It doesn't catch on in chilly Britain for another four years.) Britain gives up a huge chunk of old Victoria's Empire when Prime Minister Attlee promises India its independence.

1947 There's a coal shortage during the coldest winter since 1881. Food shortages are made worse by iced-in fishing fleets. And the Brits thought the *war* was bad. This is misery for everyone. To make school kids suffer even more, the government makes them stay at school till they're 15! Meanwhile, Britain carries out Attlee's promise and gives power back to the people of India but …

1948 Independent India suffers a terrible shock when its peace-loving leader, Mahatma Gandhi, is shot and killed by a non-peace-loving enemy. Whipping is no longer to be used as a punishment for criminals ... but beating children with a cane in school is still quite all right. A new crime is invented – hijacking – when a flying-boat is seized by Chinese bandits on its way to Hong Kong.

1949 Clothes rationing ends and 'Gorgeous Gussie' Moran plays at Wimbledon Tennis championships and shocks the crowds with flashes of lace-trimmed knickers. Britain's first launderette opens in London. Will Gorgeous Gussie use it to keep those knickers whiter than white?

Spy catchers and spy scratchers

During World War II there were posters all over the place. 'Careless talk costs lives!' and 'Walls have ears!' The messages meant the same ... 'Beware, there are German spies everywhere.'

81

Some people took this message very seriously. Very, very seriously. And a group of public schoolboys in the south of England took it so seriously they suspected nearly everyone of being a spy. This led to a very unfortunate incident in one junior public school …

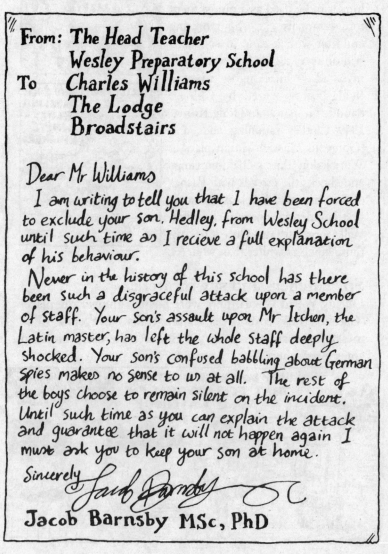

From: **The Head Teacher**
      Wesley Preparatory School
To   **Charles Williams**
      The Lodge
      Broadstairs

Dear Mr Williams

 I am writing to tell you that I have been forced to exclude your son, Hedley, from Wesley School until such time as I recieve a full explanation of his behaviour.

 Never in the history of this school has there been such a disgraceful attack upon a member of staff. Your son's assault upon Mr Itchen, the Latin master, has left the whole staff deeply shocked. Your son's confused babbling about German spies makes no sense to us at all. The rest of the boys choose to remain silent on the incident. Until such time as you can explain the attack and guarantee that it will not happen again I must ask you to keep your son at home.

Sincerely

Jacob Barnsby MSc, PhD

From: Charles Williams
      The Lodge
      Broadstairs
To: The Head Teacher
    Wesley preparatory school
Date: 16th January 1941

Dear Mr Barnsby

Thank you for your letter of 13th January. May I explain?

I'm sure you are aware that this country is full of German spies. The fearful thing is that they speak perfect English and are masters of disguise. Anyone could be a German spy.

The boys of the third form decided some action was needed to identify and arrest these spies before they did any harm. Of course the boys had very little help in identifying spies. The boys had just one reliable guide — The "Hotspur" comic.

This esteemed publication recently produced a story about a German spy and the evil man was clearly pictured in the drawings. The boys recognised him at once — the spy in the pictures looked identical to Mr Itchen, their Latin teacher. Then my son noticed something peculiar about Mr Itchen. His skin. It is very pasty, almost like putty. He was convinced that it was a fiendish German mask!

"One of us must rip the mask from his face!" my son suggested. "I will do it!" my brave little Hedley said.

Word got around that in the next Latin lesson my gallant son would tackle the German spy, Herr von Itchen (as they began to call him)

After lunch, without pausing to think of his

own life, my little Hedley leapt from the front row and dug his fingers into Mr Itchen's face. Of course, he very quickly realised that this was in fact Mr Itchen's face and not a mask.

I can quite understand why Mr. Itchen felt it necessary to run out the door. Especially since there were forty boys screaming "Spy!" at him. It is really not Mr Itchen's fault that he looks so much like the spy in "The Hotspur". It is not little Hedley's fault that he is so desperately keen to do the right thing for his country.

If you allow my son to return to school then I think we will promise he will never again attack a teacher until he has explained his suspicions to you first.

My wife and I hope that Mr Itchen is recovering from the attack. (We understand that he is presently in hospital and being treated for a complaint of the nerves. Please pass on our regrets and best wishes to him.

Your humble servant

In fact the headmaster was so totally confused by what had happened that no one was punished. (You are advised *not* to try this sort of thing in your own classroom even if your teacher is as ugly as King Kong's uncle.)

Gutsy girls

Girls were being encouraged to toughen up in the war, too. The *Girls' Own Paper* magazine had praised Adolf Hitler's German Girls' League as 'the greatest in the world' in the 1930s. Then they changed their minds.

By 1945 the *Girls' Own Paper* was running a serial story with 18-year-old heroine Joan Worralson (nicknamed Worrals).

Worrals hunted down spies, shot down German fighter-

planes, murdered a German guard and rescued prisoners of war.
She fought rats, sharks, crocodiles and tigers before recovering
with a packet of raisins or a bar of chocolate. (Chocolate was
rationed, but she'd deserved a treat, hadn't she?)

Worrals talked tough ... 'I'll shoot you, you scum. I've killed
better men than you.' And Worrals would have pleased Mrs
Pankhurst when she declared, 'Who started the war, anyway?
Men. Take a look at the world and see what a nice mess men
have made of it. No wonder they had to appeal to women to
help them out.'

Girls read Worrals' stories and rushed to join the
Women's Junior Air Corps. They must have been a bit
disappointed to end up packing parachutes instead of
splatting spies or wrestling with rats. Life is hardly ever as
exciting as the stories.

Wonders to win the war

During World War II there were people who had some incredibly clever ideas to help Britain win. Which of the following were actually put forward as war-winners?

1 Persuade Mr Hitler
• Simply prove to Adolf Hitler that the German people did not want a war. Take an opinion poll in Germany and present it to the German leader. When he sees how unpopular war is then he will stop.
• There is a slight problem with this idea. Anyone trying to organize such an opinion poll in 1939 Germany would probably be locked up. The answer is to send teams of opinion-poll questioners into Germany in disguise.

• Advertise for students. Disguise the students as golfers and instruct them to take opinion polls between rounds of golf.

2 Destroy Germany's oil supplies
- The Germans obtained much of their fuel from the Romanian oil fields. If the oil wells could be destroyed then German tanks, aeroplanes and ships would run out of fuel and become useless. Of course the oil fields were well defended.
- Send in a team of British commandos disguised as firemen. Give them fire-engines that are exact copies of the Romanian Fire Brigade machines.

- Get the Royal Air Force to drop one or two fire-bombs on the Romanian oil wells. When the fires start, send in the British Commando fake firemen. They could spray the fires with hoses, but more bombs would be mixed with the water-jets. The more they poured on the wells the more they would destroy!

3 Nobble the Norwegians
- Send in a small force of highly-trained men to Norway. Keep the Germans so busy defending Norway that they can't defend Germany.
- Build a special three-man snow-sledge that would travel round Norway planting bombs.
- Of course the Germans would suspect a strange vehicle like a snow-sledge, so it would have to be disguised. Disguise it as a hut and put a sign to keep out all curious

German soldiers. The sign could say, 'Officers' Toilet. For Colonels only.'

4 Sneak in soldiers
- Make a million German Army uniforms and dress British soldiers in them. Train the British to speak a little German.
- Drop the British-German soldiers behind the lines of the German-German soldiers.
- When the German-German soldiers come face to face with the British-British soldiers then the British-German soldiers pull out their weapons and shoot the German-German soldiers in the back.

5 Freeze the foe
- Mix water and wood-pulp then freeze it. You now have an incredibly tough material called 'Pykrete'. Bullets and bombs just bounce off it and it doesn't melt very easily.

• Build a fleet of aircraft-carrier ships and troop-carrying ships out of Pykrete. Sail straight into enemy ports – their bombs and bullets won't be able to stop you. Block the enemy harbours with Pykrete blocks so their ships can't get out. Spray their docks with Pykrete until they freeze up and leave the enemy navy helpless.

• Send teams of Pykrete-sprayers into Germany to freeze up the railways and the factories until Germany has to give up and surrender.

Answers: **1** True. The students went into Germany and began this task. Early results showed that the German people were in fact against war. Unfortunately the war started before the opinion poll could be completed. The students (and their golf clubs) were lucky to escape from Germany before they (and their golf clubs) ended up in a German prison! **2** True. This idea was considered after two others were rejected. The first was to send in a commando raid accompanied by dogs. The howling of the dogs would sound like Romanian wolves, the guards would run away and the commandos could then wreck the wells. The second idea was to send in the dogs first with bottles of brandy round their neck (like St Bernard dogs in Swiss mountain-rescue teams). The guards would get drunk and not be fit enough to protect the wells against the commando raid.

3 True. Trials were begun in America to build the right sort of snow-sledges. They were developed, but too late to be of any use in World War II. **4** False. This perfectly sensible plan was never even thought of. It was considered to be cheating. Fighters went around killing the enemy forces (and any women, children or old men who got in the way) but they had rules … as if this war was a game of cricket. One of the rules was that you didn't try to disguise yourself as an enemy. If you did, and if you were caught, then you would not be treated as a prisoner-of-war. You would be shot. **5** True. Pykrete (invented by Geoffrey Pyke) really worked. The British navy were so excited by the invention that Admiral Mountbatten caught Winston Churchill in his bath and dropped a lump of Pykrete in. It didn't melt. Churchill ordered more tests and a Pykrete ship sailed through a long hot summer on a Canadian lake without melting. Germany was defeated before the Pykrete fleet was built. The invention of the atom bomb made them useless after the war. Incredible, but true!

Foul food

German bombs weren't the only the horrors that Brits faced during the war, as this true story illustrates …

'Excuse me, waiter! May I see the manager?' the young man said.

'Yes, sir … nothing wrong, is there, sir?' the worried waiter asked.

'A small complaint,' the young man said with a grim smile.

The waiter shrugged, waddled through the door and returned a minute later with the manager. The manager forced a smile onto his wet lips and twisted his hands nervously. 'A problem, sir?' he whined.

'I'm a medical student,' the young man said.

'I see, sir,' the manager said but his blank face said that he didn't understand at all.

'Today I am actually taking an examination.'

'The best of luck, sir.'

The student ignored the comment and went on, 'And for weeks I have been cutting up dead animals to practise my skills.'

91

The manager's eyes widened. 'Could you keep your voice down just a little, sir. I think that sort of talk might upset the customers!'

The student raised his voice instead. 'We take animals that have been killed in the bombing. Mainly dogs and cats. In fact I am quite an expert on cats.'

'Ah ... I ... yes, I'm sure,' the manager muttered and his face turned as pale as the potato on the plate.

'So, when I come in here and order stewed rabbit I am a little bit shocked to find that you are serving me stewed cat!'

There was a clattering of chairs as diners rose to their feet. Some began muttering angrily, some looking in horror at their empty plates. Some made a dash for the toilets.

'Perhaps the chef made a mistake,' the man whined and rubbed a hand over his greasy hair.

The medical student rose to his feet and glared at the manager. 'The only mistake you made was to try to serve a dead cat to a medical student! I hope the police close you down,' he said as he strode out of the door and was followed by a charge of customers.

'The cats were already dead!' the manager cried after them. 'They were dead before we cooked them!'

The customers just ran faster.

The restaurant was fined ... but allowed to stay open for business and was very successful.

Curious crime

The war brought out the best in some people. They were heroes. Sadly it brought out the worst in others – the villains.

One particularly nasty gang used informers to report bomb incidents in rich areas. The gang arrived and pretended to help with the rescue. In fact they were robbing the dead and the unconscious victims. A Mrs Blair Hickman was stunned by a blast at the elegant Café de Paris restaurant. She woke to find someone slipping the rings from her fingers!

Restaurants serving cat weren't the only unusual wartime crime. The following sad cases could only happen in wartime, but do you think the arrests and punishments were fair?

• **Odd opinions** An elderly American lady sat in a café and moaned to the young army officer. 'I can't return home because of the war,' she sighed. 'You know, I've travelled through Europe and Germany and those German people are quite happy working for the Nazi government. In fact Hitler is a great leader and it isn't his fault that we are at war. It's Britain's fault!'

The army officer listened patiently – then reported her to the police. She was arrested, convicted of making statements 'likely to cause alarm and despondency' and sentenced to a month's hard labour – the first two weeks spent sleeping without a mattress. She was also fined £50 when a weekly pension was just about 10 shillings (50p).

• **Blackout badness** An 83-year-old man showed lights in his windows in the first days of the war when the public were terrified of air-raids. Before the police even arrived a huge crowd had gathered outside his door and began smashing his windows. 'Smash the door down!' the mob screamed. 'String him up!' The man was rescued by the police then arrested. He was frightened and confused. He said he knew little about the war and the blackout. That didn't stop the court fining him £2 – his whole pension for a month. No one in the crowd was charged.

• **Telling truths** A 23-year-old Welshman spoke at a meeting and described what had happened to his countrymen in the previous war. 'My forefathers won five Victoria Crosses. They were then called heroes. But, when they came back, what did they come back to? Why, their dirty little villages and slime. That's what the soldiers of 1940 will come back to.' He was charged with 'using insulting words and behaviour' and sentenced to three months in prison.

• **Sinful seances** A spiritualist held a seance with the parents of a dead soldier and they spoke to their son through her. She was arrested for fraud – even though many people said she was genuine. The magistrates did not like the idea of someone cashing in on the death and misery produced by the war. It was a little difficult to know what to charge the spiritualist with. Eventually she was charged under the Witchcraft Act of 1735 and sent to prison.

• **Straying sailors** Foreigners had to come and go from Britain during the war, but they were treated with great suspicion. No foreigner was allowed on the streets after 10:30 p.m. Foreign sailors risked their lives by sailing through waters full of German submarines. They brought food and supplies to Britain ... then were arrested if they stayed out too late. Two Greek sailors went for a drink then tried to find their way back to their ship. They became lost. 'We're all right. Here is a police station,' one said. They walked in. 'Excuse me. Can you tell us the way back to the docks?' the sailor asked politely. The policeman glared at them. 'It's 10:45 and you are not on your ship. I am arresting you!' They were fined £10 each.

Patriotic poems

It was 1946 and the music halls were filled with people celebrating the end of the war. A popular piece was in praise of the people who helped Britain to win. One of the verses went like this ...

Thank you

In this glorious hour of victory, when the world at last is free,
Free for ever from the shackles of a hateful tyranny,
In the midst of our rejoicing, let us pause a while and think
Of those to whom we owe so much, who brought us from the brink.
Let us think of them today, and of our overwhelming debt,
And say a simple 'Thank you' lest we all too soon forget.
And over all, forever shining in undying fame,
We thank you, Winston Churchill – blessed forever be your name!

… which is curious when you remember that in the election held after the war the people voted to throw Winston Churchill's party *out* of government! Maybe they should have added a couple of extra lines …

> *We thank you Winston Churchill – our champion in the fight.*
> *But now we've won, it's cheerio, goodbye and nighty night!*

Churchill's Conservatives were beaten by Clement Attlee and his Labour Party. The Labour Party promised that they would take over large businesses like coal-mining and railways. The railways would no longer be owned by the railway companies. They would be kept going by the ordinary taxpayer – owned by the British people. Imagine the thrill for all of those train-spotters! They would now own a real, live, full-size train set!

By 1995 the Conservative government decided to sell the railways back to railway companies. Train-spotters all over the country will have tears running down their anoraks. They aren't sad for too long though, in 2002 Network Rail take over the running of Britain's railways again.

The Fat Fifties

By now television has been around for over 20 years, but it becomes really popular in the Fifties. And a new breed of human is created! Before there had been just children and adults ... now there are these in-betweenies called 'teenagers'. Meanwhile another breed is disappearing – there are only a quarter of the servants that there used to be in the 1930s. By the end of the Fifties the Prime Minister (Harold Macmillan) is boasting that Brits are so well off they have 'never had it so good.' But people are worried by the nuclear bombs that finished off World War II. Russia was on the side of Britain and America during that war. Now they're afraid of one another. No fighting – just the fear of it. It's known as a 'Cold War'.

Timeline – 1950s

1950 More petrol is available at last, so rationing ends. 4.5 million drivers take to the roads ... and huge holiday traffic-jams start!

1951 Exciting television programmes include *For The Housewife* which tells the viewers the best way to cook whale meat and how to grow your own tobacco. (No doubt you are sorry you missed these delights.)

1952 Television fury over a new children's programme! Bill and Ben 'The Flowerpot Men' talk in a strange 'fer-lub-a-lub' language. Parents object that this is setting their children a bad example. The BBC statement as usual says, 'Fer-lub-a-lub-a-lub-a-lub.'

1953 Queen Elizabeth II crowned – 526,000 families rush out to buy television sets to watch the coronation, making a total of 2,500,000 sets in the country. 20 million people claimed to have watched the coronation. That's about eight people to every set. Winston Churchill (now back in power for a while) doesn't like the idea of television at a coronation but Elizabeth insists – she wants her sick granny to be able to watch her being crowned. First tea-bags in Britain.

1954 Britain's clever inventors invent myxomatosis. It's a disease that kills off that vicious pest – the rabbit. Unfortunately they can't come up with a disease to kill off the vicious new human pests called Teddy Boys (tough youths with grease in their hair who dress in long jackets and 'drainpipe' trousers). Brave Brit Roger Bannister is the first man in history to run a mile in less than four minutes. (He was probably being chased by an angry rabbit at the time.) Meat rationing ends – the last rationed food after 14 years.

1955 Fish fingers are invented and Winston Churchill retires. (Is there a connection? you might well ask!) Equal pay for women but equal punishments too. Ruth Ellis is

hanged for murder – the last woman to be executed in Britain. 'The Harmful Publications Act' is a law aimed at protecting children from violent comics! (Have you ever been attacked by a 'violent comic'?)

1956 Weird music called 'rock and roll' comes to Britain from America. The rockers flock to cinemas to see *Rock Around the Clock* and cause riots. 'Pop' music has arrived and the world will never be the same again. Europe strikes back with the Eurovision Song Contest – not quite the same thing. The first yellow no-parking lines appear on roads. Britain sends forces to crush Egypt when that country takes control of the Suez Canal. British troops fail miserably. Very embarrassing – another blow to Brits' fading empire.

1957 The Russians send their first astronaut into space … a dog called Laika. The Americans are in second place in the 'space race' when their rocket gets half-a-metre off the ground. President Eisenhower of the USA is so upset he tells the world, 'I am not worried!' (But everyone knows he is!) The Americans' only space-travel answer is to invent the Frisbee! (It's based on an 1871 American game of skimming empty pie-dishes after eating a Frisbie Pie.)

1958 Traffic slowed down by new speed limits and then the dreaded parking meters hit the streets. Soon someone will have to invent a traffic warden to check them! The rule for towns is, 'If it moves, stop it; if it stops, fine it.'

1959 The Americans send two monkeys into space and get them back alive … then they operate to remove electrical connections from one – and kill it! Meanwhile the Russians send a rocket round the moon and take pictures of the back of the moon to prove it. Russia – 2: America – 0 in the space race. At least an American woman, Bertha Dlugi, restores America's pride. She invents The Bird Nappy to stop your pet parrot pooping on your pepperpot. And, most important, American doll Barbie is born.

I'm sitting on top of the world

Stupid question number 368: Chomolungma used to be the highest mountain in the world. Now it is Mount Everest. What happened to Chomolungma?

Stupid (but true) answer: the British *changed its name* in 1856. Sir George Everest made the first map of the mountain so they named the 8,850-metre pile of rock after him and printed it on all their maps of the world. The British didn't ask the native people of Tibet if they could change the name of their holy mountain. (They never do.) The Tibetans got their own back – they refused to let the Brits climb their Chomolungma (which means Mother-Goddess) for the next 60 years. This was incredibly kind and probably saved dozens of mountaineers' lives.

Then, in 1920, they finally gave permission for Brits to boldly go where no man or woman had ever boldly gone before ... to the top of Chomolungma.

The Royal Geographical Society (for explorers and all that) formed the Everest Committee. First they appealed for money ... they raised just £10. At last they found some people with more money than sense and sent off expeditions in 1921, 1922 and 1924 to see how far they could get.

The 1921 expedition got to within a mile of the summit but Chomolungma started to get its revenge ...

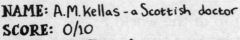

CHOMOLUNGMA CASEBOOK 1

NAME: A.M. Kellas - a Scottish doctor

SCORE: 0/10

ACHIEVEMENT: The first victim of attempts to climb Chomolungma. Died on 1921 expedition before he got within a hundred miles.

QUOTE: Sir Francis Younghusband of the Everest Committee said "Kellas remained cheery and no one considered there was anything critically serious with him." Kellas was too ill to walk or even ride a yak. He was so ill he had to be carried... but he wasn't considered "critically serious"!

MIGHT SAY: "A lot of idiots may die on this mountain - but remember, I was first!"

WOULDN'T SAY: "Put me down chaps, so I can do the last 100 miles on foot."

The 1922 expedition went to Chomolungma and climbed higher still. It ended when seven of the Tibetan guides were swept away by an avalanche. Still the climbers came back for more ...

CHOMOLUNGMA CASEBOOK 2

NAME: George Leigh Mallory - a school teacher!

SCORE: 5/10

ACHIEVEMENT: He climbed in 1921 and 1922. In 1924 he climbed higher than anyone before... then vanished into a cloud and was never seen again. (Not even his body.)

QUOTE: Mallory wrote after the first expedition, "Mount Everest, as it turned out, did not prove difficult to find." Imagine that! He managed to find the world's largest mountain even though he was a school teacher! When he was asked why he wanted to climb the mountain he answered "Because it is there!" (You may like to try this excuse next time a teacher asks you why you broke a window with your football or why you hit him on the back of the head with an ink pellet.) The truth is he climbed the mountain because he hoped the publicity would get him a better teaching job!

MIGHT SAY: "A teacher's gotta do what a teacher's gotta do!"

WOULDN'T SAY: "A helicopter would come in handy!"

The Tibetans banned any more attempts until 1933. That didn't stop the slightly crazy Lady Fanny Houston giving money towards the first flight over Chomolungma. As the expedition passed the top of the mountain they dropped a flag. A Union Jack was the first flag on top of Chomolungma ... but some people might think that was cheating just a bit.

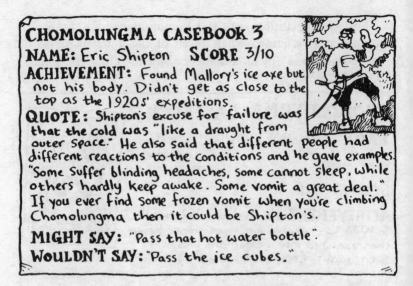

CHOMOLUNGMA CASEBOOK 3
NAME: Eric Shipton   **SCORE** 3/10
ACHIEVEMENT: Found Mallory's ice axe but not his body. Didn't get as close to the top as the 1920s' expeditions.
QUOTE: Shipton's excuse for failure was that the cold was "like a draught from outer space." He also said that different people had different reactions to the conditions and he gave examples. "Some suffer blinding headaches, some cannot sleep, while others hardly keep awake. Some vomit a great deal." If you ever find some frozen vomit when you're climbing Chomolungma then it could be Shipton's.
MIGHT SAY: "Pass that hot water bottle".
WOULDN'T SAY: "Pass the ice cubes."

Expeditions failed but one individual went it alone. In 1934 Maurice Wilson first planned to crash-land a plane near the top of the mountain then scramble up the last few metres – his aeroplane was confiscated. He then said that starving your body would make it pure and your pure spirit could race up the mountainside. So Wilson set off with some rice-water, a Union Jack to stick on the top and a few sherpas (guides). The sensible sherpas deserted him at 6,400 metres. Two years later his body and his diary were found.

After World War II a shocking thing happened. A group from Switzerland set off to beat the Brits to the top! The Swiss failed – the Brits celebrated the Swiss failure (which was a bit cruel) and Sir John Hunt led an expedition in 1953.

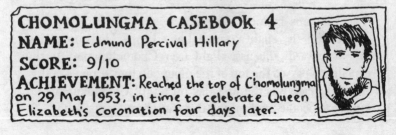

CHOMOLUNGMA CASEBOOK 4
NAME: Edmund Percival Hillary
SCORE: 9/10
ACHIEVEMENT: Reached the top of Chomolungma on 29 May 1953, in time to celebrate Queen Elizabeth's coronation four days later.

Of course the Queen gave him a knighthood.

QUOTE: Hillary said, "It is not the mountain we conquer but ourselves," which is a very wise thing to say. The conquered Chomolungma was even wiser and said nothing. In the argument over who stood on top first – him or guide Tenzing – he said "On a tight rope from Tenzing I climbed up a gentle snow ridge to it's top." That sounds as if the Tibetan guide got there first.

MIGHT SAY: "I'm the king of the castle and you're a dirty rascal!"

WOULDN'T SAY: "Everest today... 'ave a rest tomorrow."

CHOMOLUNGMA CASEBOOK 5

NAME: Norkay Tenzing – Tibetan guide
('Sherpa')

SCORE 10/10

ACHIEVEMENT: Reached the top of Chomolungma with Hillary but had probably got there first and hauled Hillary up after him. He had been climbing and guiding people for twenty years before that. Of course the Queen didn't give him a knighthood. He had to make do with a George Medal.

QUOTE: Hillary took Tenzing's photo on the top of Everest. Tenzing did not take Hillary's picture. Hillary explained "As far as I know he had never taken a photo before and the summit of Everest was hardly the place to show him how." Tenzing wrote a book about his adventure (even though he couldn't read or write!) The Nepalese thought he was a much greater hero than the British expedition leaders and wanted to rename Chomolungma as Tenzing Mountain. Brit leader John Hunt was not amused. "Tenzing was nothing at all" he announced a bit spitefully.

MIGHT SAY: "What does it matter who got there first?"

WOULDN'T SAY: "Give us a hand up, Ed!"

After the nasty arguments about who got there first it shouldn't have really mattered to Britain in the end. Neither Hillary nor Tenzing were British, were they?

Then, amazingly, on 22 May 1995 George Mallory reached the top of Mount Everest. No, not the ghost of George Leigh Mallory. No, not the old man himself with his map turned the right way up at last. It was his grandson who had boldly gone where Grandad had boldly gone before and finally put a Mallory on the Mount – 71 years later.

AND ABOUT TIME TOO!

Television times

In the Fifties television 'arrived' in a big way. Now everybody knows about television. But you can still paralyse your parents or gobsmack your granny with these incredible facts. Say ...

Did you know...?

• Television started before World War II but closed down for the six war years. When it started again in June 1946, the announcer began by saying, 'As I was saying before we were so rudely interrupted ...'

• A popular Fifties quiz game was called *What's my line?*. Four 'experts' had to guess a person's job. One man appeared and claimed he was a frogman (diver). A bank manager was watching and recognized him as the man who passed forged cheques in his bank. The police were informed and the frogman got 15 months in jail before he could hop it.

• Most early programmes were shown 'live'. Mistakes and accidents had to be shown as they happened. In a show called *Fast and Loose* the comedian Bob Monkhouse fired blanks at fellow comedian Charlie Drake. The packing from the blanks blew off half of Charlie Drake's ear! He finished the scene, had his ear stitched and came back to take his bow at the end of the show. None of the viewers noticed!

• The George Orwell book, *Nineteen Eighty-Four*, was turned into a television play in 1954. One nasty scene needed sewer rats to threaten a man – but the sewer rats fainted in the hot studio lights. The director brought in tame rats from a local pet shop, but they were the wrong colour. They were white and they should have been brown. The make-up department dyed them brown!

OF COURSE LUVVIE, IT'S NOT JUST A QUESTION OF DYEING YOURSELF BROWN, OH NO, YOU REALLY HAVE TO *THINK* LIKE A SEWER RAT...

• Even by 1965 many programmes were still going out live and causing problems. The comedian Jimmy Tarbuck had to introduce singer Petula Clark on a live show … then completely forgot her name! What would you have done? Jimmy simply said, 'Now here is someone who needs no introduction …' and walked off the stage.

• In a 1957 programme called *The Sky at Night* the presenter, Patrick Moore, opened his mouth to speak and a fly flew in. The programme, like the fly, was live. What should he do? Spit it out in front of millions of viewers? No! He quickly closed his mouth, gave a sharp swallow and carried on. He later told his family about this horrible experience. He got no sympathy. 'It was worse for the fly,' his mother told him.

• Another comedian with a problem was Tony Hancock. He had to record a half-hour episode of his comedy series about a blood donor. He nearly needed blood himself when he was in a car crash shortly before the recording. He made it to the studios but had no time to learn his lines. Instead, the lines were written on 'idiot boards' for him to read. If you ever see a video of this show you'll notice that he never looks at any other characters. He's looking over their shoulders at his words. He enjoyed this so much he never learned words again!

• *Blue Peter* could be an even more dangerous programme to appear on. Apart from danger to the presenters (John Noakes ended up in hospital when knocked out by a 2kg imitation marrow) there were dangers for guests. A guest tortoise celebrated its 100th birthday on *Blue Peter* and was greeted by Mark Curry ... who promptly stepped on him.

AND HERE'S ONE I STEPPED ON EARLIER...

• Everyone knows television can give you harmful ideas. The 'Twist' dance was banned from a television programme in 1962 because a doctor said it just might cause ankle sprains. And you are often warned, 'Children do not try this at home. Only Superman can jump off a settee and live!' But no warning came in the 1961 programme *Candid Camera*. A joker swallowed a piece of goldfish-shaped carrot in a pet shop fish-tank – hidden cameras captured the horrified expressions of customers. They thought it was a live fish. A viewer phoned to complain when her young son toddled into the next room ... and ate their goldfish!

• By 1965 most television programmes were recorded. Mistakes could be corrected before the public saw them. A word-game programme called *Call My Bluff* had two teams guessing the meanings of unusual words. The chairman was Robert Robinson, who had to ask the team to guess the meaning of 'kerseymere'. Unfortunately the word proved difficult to pronounce. As he said it his false teeth jumped out and landed on the desk in front of him. Sadly that scene was cut.

Puzzle your parents

Parents, grandparents and other wrinklies will always say things like, 'When I was your age television was much better. None of these "Sponge Bob Square Trousers" and "The Sampsons". We had proper programmes in them days!'

If you can stop their whingeing for long enough then you could say, 'Then maybe you could answer a few questions about Fifties and Sixties television?'

They will get most of the answers wrong. Shake your head, sigh, and say, 'Of course it was all a very long time ago …'

1 *Andy Pandy*. First shown in 1950 and ran until 1970. How many Andy Pandy programmes were made?
a) 26
b) 260
c) 2600

2 *Billy Bunter.* Ran for ten years from 1952. Gerald Campion played the part of 16-year-old Billy Bunter even though his real age was …
a) 9
b) 19
c) 29

3 Animal heroes. In the 1950s 'Lassie' was the number-one heroine. But there were other heroes and heroines. Which is the odd one out?
a) Rin-Tin-Tin
b) Lenny the Lion
c) Champion the Wonder Horse

4 Long-distance soap *Coronation Street* started in 1960 and became a national favourite. But it was meant to be called …
a) Florizel Street
b) Corporation Street
c) Acacia Avenue

I WISH THEY'D MAKE THEIR MINDS UP!

5 Short Sheriff Tex Tucker was a puppet sheriff of *Four Feather Falls*. Two magic feathers allowed his guns to fire automatically when he was in danger. What did the other two feathers do?
a) Tickle his enemies until they screamed for mercy and surrendered.

b) Attach themselves to the wings of a bird and fly off to track down crooks.

c) Give his horse and dog the power to talk to Tex and help him out.

Answers: **1 a)** Only 26 *Andy Pandy* programmes were ever made. They were repeated endlessly for 20 years. **2 c)** And by the end of the series he was 39. Of course it was only fair that a boy should be played by an adult. After all, adults enjoyed the programme too. It was shown at 5:30 p.m. for children then repeated two hours later for parents. And it was a very adult show with Billy Bunter swearing so much! A vicar once complained that Bunter said that naughty word 'Crikey!' 13 times in half an hour. **3 b)** Lenny the Lion was a puppet. The others were trained animals. For a bonus point you could ask what was Lenny's famous catch-phrase? Answer, 'Aw! Don't embarrass me!' (He was probably embarrassed because the ventriloquist, Terry Hall, had his arm stuck up the lion's bum.) **4 a)** The writer, Tony Warren, called it *Florizel Street* but they asked a television tea-lady for her opinion. 'Sounds like a sort of disinfectant,' she sniffed. They changed it. They broadcast it and a newspaper wrote the next day, 'The programme is doomed.' Wrong! **5 c)** The four feathers were given to Tex by an Indian. Dusty the Dog and Rocky the Horse enjoyed their little chats when they were stroked by the magic feathers. Fortunately these feathers are not available in shops today. Imagine your dog telling you what it wants for dinner … or your horse swearing at car drivers who speed past!

The Swinging Sixties

The Sixties become known as the 'Swinging Sixties'. Suddenly those teenagers of the Fifties have begun to influence the world and turn it upside down. Women wear short skirts and men have long hair. Lots of jobs and young people with money to spend on records and clothes. But it doesn't stop the Cold War from getting colder – the Russians shut the East Germans behind the Berlin Wall.

Timeline – 1960s

1960 America invents the 'Twist' dance while Britain has to make do with pop songs like *My Old Man's A Dustman*. America fights back with the super-cool *Itsy-bitsy-teeny-weeny-yellow-polka-dot-bikini*. Britain invents ready-salted crisps. As grimly predicted back in 1958, the traffic warden is invented – known affectionately as the 'Yellow Peril' because of the yellow band round the uniform hat (and the disgusting disease of that name!).

1961 Now the Russians send the first human into space. Major Yuri Gagarin comes back alive (unlike Laika the dog who went up before him). Space Race score: Russia – 3: America – 0. In Britain suicide is no longer a crime – when the law was made in 1854 you could be hanged if you tried to commit suicide!

1962 The Brits can't quite manage a spaceship – but they do agree with France to build a supersonic airliner called *Concorde*. Will it ever fly? Yes! Will it ever make a profit? No.

1963 American President Kennedy assassinated. He told the American people they would have the first man on the moon. He won't be alive to see it. Meanwhile the Russians send the first woman into space. Britain sees The Great Train Robbery and cassette tape-recorders. Britain invaded (on television at least) by evil wheelie-bins called Daleks.

1964 Britain invades America … with four young men called The Beatles! Their weapons? Pop music. (At least the Brits can do something right.) The Americans reply by sending the incredible Sindy Doll over here. She has British boy 'Action Man' to keep her company (or run her over in his Action Jeep). In South Africa the government locks up a man called Nelson Mandela and will keep him locked up for 25 years. His real crime is to fight for equal rights for the black people in his country.

1965 Shocking young women wear something called the 'mini-skirt'. Sir Winston Churchill dies (no connection). There is a 70 m.p.h. speed limit on roads and police Panda cars to catch the villains who dare to go faster. Home video-recorders are on sale and within 20

years some people will know how to use them properly.

1966 England's football team win the World Cup. They beat Germany in the final. This is a bit unfair because they have beaten Germany in two wars. It's about time they let the Germans win.

1967 Water year! Brit disaster when Donald Campbell is killed trying to break the world water-speed record on Lake Coniston. Slower and steadier Brit Francis Chichester is the first man to sail around the world by himself. Posher and smoother, the liner *Queen Elizabeth II* is launched.

1968 The post office invents first- and second-class postage. One is really slow but the other is incredibly slower. American astronauts fly round moon and come back without landing on it. (Must have been sent third-class post.)

1969 Americans land on the moon. They announce it is *not* made of green cheese and fly home. Egyptian Radio calls it 'the greatest human achievement ever'. (The builders of their pyramids probably disagree.) At least the Brits get *Concorde* off the ground. (The second greatest human achievement ever?) Then Brits finally get into orbit when America sends … the *Star Trek* TV series! Those teenagers get the vote when the voting age is lowered to 18.

The high life

In the Sixties the rebuilding of the country after World War II was racing away. The old slums were knocked down ... and replaced by new slums! The difference was that the new houses piled people on top of each other in high-rise flats. These caused as many problems as the old terraced slums and a few new problems too. They didn't solve the problem of poverty. One old woman thought she had an answer to her problem. Her social worker told this story ...

'I want to sell my body,' Mrs Wilson said.

At first I thought I'd misheard her. Did she say 'body'? Or was it 'Bobby'? Maybe a cat called Bobby that she wanted to sell.

'I'll see if I can help you,' I murmured as I scrubbed at her windows with a duster. I wasn't a cleaner, you understand. I was sent to see if she needed any help. 'Me windows could do with a clean,' she had said.

116

She lived on the 25th floor of a grim, grey block of flats. I could have called the council cleaning department, but I decided to do the job myself. First I cleaned the insides then I swung the window open to clean the outside. I made the mistake of looking down and froze with fear at the sight of the drop. The clear, cold air tugged at my hair and seemed to drag me over the edge. I closed my eyes and tried to steady myself. Somehow I cleaned the window with my eyes closed, swung it shut and tottered back into the room.

At least the fresh air had let some of the smell out of the room. The sickening sweet smell of Mrs Wilson's bed. She explained as soon as I walked in the door, 'Sorry about the smell, love. I wet the bed, you see.'

I arranged for the council to deliver a new mattress, cleaned that window and offered to make us a cup of tea. 'I never wanted to move here, you know,' she sighed. 'I had one of those little terraced houses near the town centre,' she explained. 'They knocked it down to build the new shopping centre. They say it's very nice.'

117

The new centre was a bleak and windswept tangle of tunnels that trapped litter and dirt in swirling piles. 'You've never been there, then?'

'Can't get out much,' she sighed. 'My toenails need cutting so I've a bit of trouble walking. Last time I went down in the lift I came back to find it was broken. I had to wait three hours for them to fix it.'

'Couldn't they find you a flat on the ground floor?' I asked.

Mrs Wilson shrugged. 'I wrote and asked. They said the ground floor was for disabled tenants. I didn't qualify. Looks like I'm stuck here till the day I die.'

I made a note to send someone round to cut her toenails and to try again for a ground-floor flat.

'Can I make us that cup of tea?' I asked.

'That's kind of you, pet. You'll find the stuff in the kitchen cabinets.'

When I opened the cabinets the boxes fell out. Toys and dolls and games. Easter eggs, gone soft and mouldy with

age. She stood in the doorway, watching. 'Presents for the grandchildren,' she said. 'Me son Eddie. His kids.'

'Don't you ever see him to give them the presents?' I asked as I tried to push the mess back into the cupboard.

'Me and Eddie had a row one Christmas Day – he'd had a bit too much to drink,' she explained. 'I went to see him on Boxing Day but he slammed the door in my face. That was seven years ago and he hasn't spoken to me since. I still buy presents for the kids,' she smiled. 'One day I might be able to give them. The teabags are in the oven, by the way. They're safe from the damp in there.'

When we sat down at the table with the cracked mugs between us she looked up at me shyly and said, 'I want you to sell my body.'

I think my mouth fell open and I said something stupid like, 'You what?'

'Doctors have bodies to practise on, don't they? I thought that I could sell my body to them and the money could give me a decent burial when I've finished.'

119

The tea seemed bitter as I supped at it and tried to think. 'Why would you want to do a thing like that?' I asked.

'My Eddie would have to pay for me funeral otherwise. I don't want the lad to have the expense,' she said.

I felt my anger rise against this man that I'd never met. 'He hasn't even spoken to you for the last seven years,' I cried.

She looked at me blankly as if I were stupid. 'What's that got to do with anything?' she asked. 'He's family. It's not fair to saddle him with a big bill like that. Sell me body – that's the best thing!'

And I tried. No one was interested. They had plenty to practise on. Unless she had some rare disease, they said, they wouldn't give a penny. In Mrs Wilson's eyes I was a failure. 'Sold it yet?' was the first thing she asked every time I saw her.

'Not yet,' I had to admit. 'Not ever,' was the truth.

I was new to social work. Mrs Wilson was one of my first cases. She was also my last. It got so that I couldn't bear to face her little blue eyes peering up at me and asking, 'Have you sold it yet?'

I'd joined the service to help people. I'd failed. I went back to the office and handed in my resignation.

Sorry, Mrs Wilson. Sorry.

Strange ... but true

The Oxo cubes that Scott took to the Antarctic found a sudden new popularity in the 1960s! In 1967 the breathalyser was used as a test for motorists to see if they had been drinking. Anyone who drank too much would lose their licence. Then a sensational story went around. Pop an Oxo cube into your last drink – preferably gin – and drink it. You would then beat the breathalyser (as long as a drink of gin and Oxo didn't make you vomit into the nearest bucket). You would not breathe out alcohol, you would breathe out oxygen ... or Oxo-gin!

You will be pleased to hear that the people who believed this (and tried it) failed the breathalyser test and lost their licences.

Manic music

Ask any wrinklies that you know and they'll tell you, 'The Sixties had the best music.' Their eyes go all glassy as they travel back in time to those golden days.

They may even bore you with some of their memories.

'Woodstock!' they exclaim. (This was a pop festival held in 1969 and about 50 million wrinklies attended it – if you believe all the people who say they were there. The truth is about 49.6 million of those only dreamed they were there.)

'*A Whiter Shade of Pale!*' they cry.

You exclaim, 'That's a new range of Dulux emulsion paint, isn't it? Saw it advertised on the telly!'

Now it's the time to burst the balloon of their dreams as they ramble on about the Sixties and Seventies 'classic' songs.

1. The Cougars, 1963
2. Charlie Drake, 1961
3. Rufus Thomas, 1970
4. Marvin Gaye, 1969

5. Bobby 'Boris' Pickett and the Crypt Kickers, 1973
6. UK group in 1972
7. Wayne Fontana and the Mindbenders, 1964
8. Napoleon XIV, 1966
9. Engelbert Humperdinck, 1967
10. Sung by Scatman John. Reached number four in June 1995.

123

Foul and funny facts

The Sixties were famous for their pop music. The tasteless tales from the world of pop are typical of the last half of the 20th century. Tough, ruthless, funny and above all wild and youthful. But which of these tacky tales is true?

1 In 1960 singer/songwriter Roy Orbison also cashed in on a bit of misery. He wrote a song called *It's Too Soon to Know (If I Can Forget Her)* about his wife, Claudette. What had Claudette done?
a) Left Roy to go and live with Cliff Richard.
b) Killed herself in a motorcycle accident.
c) Gone to prison for shoplifting.

2 Not everyone took life so seriously. In the 1967 Beatles song *Strawberry Fields Forever*, the lead singer, John Lennon, can be heard muttering as the music fades. What is he muttering?
a) Strawberry jam, strawberry jam, strawberry jam.
b) Cranberry sauce, cranberry sauce, cranberry sauce.
c) Get your drum off my foot, Ringo!

3 In the tasteless Grandmaster Flash record, *The Message*, what were the dramatic lyrics?
a) They pushed that girl in front of the train / took her to the doctor, sewed her arm on again.

b) Don't jump off the roof, dad / you'll make a hole in the yard.

c) Help! I need somebody, help! Not just anybody, help!

4 Pop star Gary Glitter was famous for his high platform boots and even higher hairstyle. One night he jumped into a swimming pool at a party. He thought the water would come up to his waist. In fact he had jumped in the *deep* end. What disturbing effect did this have on him?

a) He almost drowned but was rescued and given the kiss of life by a fan. He dedicated his 1981 hit *And Then She Kissed Me* to her.

b) As he shot to the surface his swimming trunks came off and revealed a tattoo which said, 'I love my Mum'.

c) His wig was washed off to reveal his totally bald head.

5 Singer Sam Cooke was a friend of heavyweight boxing champ, Muhammed Ali. He was also as fast on his feet until one night in 1964 he was hit by something faster. What?

a) A Greyhound bus when he jumped into the road to wave it down.

b) A bullet from the gun of a woman he'd upset.

c) A brick dropped from the roof of a skyscraper.

6 The British rock group *The Who* were famous for smashing up their instruments on stage after their performance. They also had another nasty habit. What?
a) Spitting at each other during the performance.
b) Throwing their dirty socks into the audience.
c) Singing *God Save the Queen* backwards.

7 In the Sixties pop singers often became involved with strange mystic religions. Sometimes their religious leaders went on stage with them! One Brit singer, Dave Berry, told his audience he would return to this life after he died. But *what* would he return as?
a) A snake.
b) A lawn mower.
c) A singer with a tuneful voice.

Answers: **1 b) 2 b)** It's a fact. Find a wrinkly who owns this record and listen for yourself. **3 a)** It was banned by some radio stations. Record b) (a Tommy Cooper record of 1961) was never banned. Record c) was a Beatles record. **4 c)** Luckily he didn't have his famous platform shoes on or he would still be stuck at the bottom. **5 b)** He died, by the way. One of his greatest songs was *You Send Me*. She did that all right. **6 a)** They also used to fight with each other on stage. **7 a)** He used to twine himself around the microphone like a snake.

The Sinister Seventies

The Seventies are definitely un-swinging after the Sixties. Brit government blames a huge rise in oil prices for sending the price of everything else up – most things cost five times as much as they had in the Forties. Jobs are harder to find as computers do the work of several humans in a fraction of the time. The Seventies start with peace and love from something called 'Flower Power' ... love your enemy and give him a bunch of daffodils. The Seventies ended with punks ... hate everybody and give your enemy a bunch of fives (not pound notes, either)!

Timeline – 1970s

1970 'Troublesome' women are being 'troublesome' again. They disrupt the 'Miss World' competition. These new 'troublesome' women are this time not suffragettes but are into 'Women's Lib' (short for liberation). 'Troublesome' young men cut their hair and call themselves 'Skinheads'.

1971 The Americans drive a buggy on the Moon. Back on Earth a British government minister upsets a lot of parents by stopping free school milk for children. The minister is nicknamed 'Milk-snatcher' because it rhymes with her name ... Thatcher. A name to remember (if you can bear to)!

1972 Brit inventor Clive Sinclair invents the pocket calculator. Schoolchildren everywhere see an end to those terrible multiplication tables. At least, those with a spare £79 … because that's how much the new calculator costs!

1973 A war in the Middle East cuts oil supplies to Britain. Suddenly the Brits discover how much they need the stuff. Car speed limits cut to 50 m.p.h. (to save fuel) and many factories cut work to just three days a week. Sadly, schools hardly affected.

1974 The laws are changed to make women equal – anyone who refuses to give a woman a job just because she's a woman will face legal action – a fine or prison. But some people still treat it as a bit of a joke. One newspaper says, 'There will be exceptions. The army won't have to employ dolly girls on the front line.' (Sensible women would like to see sexist journalists 'on the front line' … and being shot at for such remarks!) Meanwhile, a Japanese soldier (male) walks out of a Philippine jungle and gives himself up – no one told him the war had ended 19 years before. (He was very happy to collect his back pay!)

1975 The film *Jaws* terrifies people at the cinema while Mrs Thatcher terrifies Conservatives into electing her as their leader. Of course the British people would never elect her as Prime Minister, would they! *Would* they?

1976 *Concorde* begins carrying passengers from London to Paris (and back, of course). The hottest summer for 200 years. Everyone says, 'Lovely weather we're having.' (No one says, 'This is Global Warming! This is the beginning of the end of the world!' No one says that … yet.) A Portsmouth teacher dies and leaves £26,000 in his will to Jesus if He 'shall return to reign on Earth'. (Other teachers ask for a pay rise!)

1977 Elvis Presley, pop singer, dies on the toilet. To make things worse a couple of thieves try to steal his body from the grave. Perhaps they should have used America's latest craze to help them … skateboards. Some people want skateboarding to become an Olympics event!

1978 A children's serial about a school begins. It's called *Grange Hill*. Teachers are horrified by the programme (are you surprised?). It's not so much the shoplifting, the smoking and the truancy. It's the fact that some pupils call teachers … by their *first* names!!! A teachers' union complains, 'The teachers are made to look like buffoons!' … so it must be fairly accurate. (That is b-u-f-f-o-o-n-s, not b-a-b-o-o-n-s.)

1979 Britain elects its first woman Prime Minister – Margaret Thatcher.

130

'Troublesome' women come out on top at last! Meanwhile the House of Lords gives Britain another 'first'. They are the first government in the world to have a debate on that vital subject – Unidentified Flying Objects!

The lucky lord

By the Seventies the power of the upper classes was far less than it had been at the start of the century. But the Lords and Ladies who remained still had one bit of power … the power to interest the rest of the people of Britain. Especially if there was a bit of scandal concerned. And it also seemed that they still had the power to get away with murder … literally. One of the most famous murder mysteries of the century involved a lord. Or did it?

They call him Lucky. It's a play on his name – Lucan. It's also because of his gambling habit. Lucky Lucan.

Officially he's a murderer – though he's never had a trial and some do not believe he did it.

Officially he's dead – though no body has ever been found and even fewer believe that.

His story …

On 7 November 1974 Lord 'Lucky' Lucan said he was driving past his wife's house in Lower Belgrave Street, London. He was hoping for a glimpse of his children. He'd been separated from his wife for a year and he missed the kids. Instead he saw something so horrific he rushed to the front door and opened it with his own key.

He had looked down to a basement window and seen a man attacking his wife. He leapt down the stairs and arrived in time to stop him murdering her. The stranger waved a blood-stained piece of lead pipe at 'Lucky' Lucan. As Lucan tried to dodge it he slipped in a pool of blood and the

131

attacker escaped into the street. He turned to calm his wife but she was hysterical. 'She accused me of being her attacker!' he told a friend later.

At midnight he rang his mother and asked her to care for the children. 'There's been a terrible catastrophe. Veronica and the nanny have been badly hurt.'

'I know. The police are here now,' his mother told him. 'Do you want to speak to them?'

'I'll ring them in the morning. I'll ring you too,' he promised. It was a promise he never kept.

He didn't expect anyone to believe him so he drove down to Newhaven – a ferry port with regular trips to France … and disappeared!

Her story …
'I was sitting at home with the children and their nanny, Sandra,' Veronica, Lady Lucan, told police. The children had been put to bed and Sandra offered to make a cup of tea for Lady Lucan. After 20 minutes Sandra had not returned with the tea. Lady Lucan went to investigate.

When she reached the basement she saw the shadowy figure of a man. He was bending over the bloodstained body of the nanny and pushing it into a large sack. She screamed, he turned and attacked her with a piece of lead pipe.

She didn't recognize him but, as she fled upstairs, it was her husband's voice she heard calling to her. As she lay half-conscious upstairs, it was her husband who was by her side. She was sure he was the attacker now. When he left the room for a moment she fled from the house, raced down the street and staggered into the Plumber's Arms public house. 'Help me!' she cried. 'Help me! I've just escaped from a murderer. He's in the house!'

The police story …
The first police to arrive on the scene found the house in darkness. Two children were asleep upstairs and one awake. In the basement kitchen was the body of Nanny Sandra, just as Lady Lucan had said.

She had been battered to death. A piece of lead pipe lay on the floor. Sticking plaster was wrapped around the handle for a better grip.

A search was organized for Lord Lucan and when his car was found the next day at Newhaven, the boot was opened. Lying there was a length of lead pipe with sticking plaster round one end. It was identical to the one used to kill Sandra.

They interviewed his friends, including ones he'd visited after the murder. Lord Lucan had told those friends his story. The police checked Lucky Lucan's story but found it wasn't possible to see into the kitchen from the street, as he'd claimed.

While the search for Lord Lucan spread, some detectives looked into his past life. He had spent so much time and money gambling that his wife had left him and taken the children with her. He had tried once before to snatch the children while they were out with their nanny. He had even tried to prove that Lady Lucan was mentally ill so the courts would put the children into his care.

At the time of the murder he was not so 'lucky' with his gambling. He owed a lot of money and was nearly bankrupt. He blamed his wife.

The explanations ...

Over the years there have been many people who have tried to explain what happened on that night. Only the killer knows the truth ... if he (or she) is still alive. Here are some of the ideas that have been put forward. There is no certain answer. You must decide for yourself.

1 Lord Lucan armed himself with a piece of lead pipe and let himself into his wife's house, planning to kill her. (He hoped the murder would stay unsolved and he would be free to look after the children.) He saw a movement in the

kitchen, went down and attacked the woman there. Too late he discovered it was the nanny and not his wife who lay dead on the floor. He changed his name and is living in some other country.

2 Lord Lucan felt he had to kill the nanny. He expected Lady Lucan to be alone since that night was Sandra's night off. Sandra had changed her mind at the last minute and stayed. She would be a witness to his crime so he had to kill her. Lady Lucan appeared and put up a stronger fight so he gave up. After he had fled he killed himself in some remote spot, ashamed of killing an innocent nanny.

3 Lord Lucan did not kill the nanny – he would never mistake her for his wife – but he did hire a paid killer to do the job. The man assumed the woman in the kitchen was Lady Lucan and murdered her. When Lord Lucan turned up to check that the job had been done he sent the hired killer away and tried to help his wife recover. When she fled for help he realized he'd have to disappear himself.

4 The whole of the police case was twisted to make Lucky Lucan appear guilty so no one would suspect the real killer. They planted the lead pipe in the boot of the car. Why? Because the nanny was killed by a *policeman!*

5 A burglar had sneaked into Lady Lucan's house while the nanny and the family were upstairs. Sandra disturbed the burglar and he killed her. Lady Lucan saw him and he attacked her. When Lord Lucan arrived the burglar fled and left his lordship to take the blame.

This case led to a change in the law. Lord Lucan was found *guilty* of murder even though he had not been brought to trial. This can no longer happen.

Mystery of the moors

The Seventies didn't only see crime mysteries. They saw mysteries of the supernatural, too. That debate in the House of Lords about UFOs was just one sample of the interest in the unexplained.

DID THE HAIRY HANDS HOLD THE GHOSTLY SECRET OF AN ANCIENT EXECUTIONER... OR ONE OF HIS VICTIMS?

Florence was lucky. She lived to tell the tale. By the Seventies humans had explored most of this planet and even the moon – yet they couldn't explain simple incidents ...

The spooky Seventies

The Seventies were a great time for students of the 'unexplained'. Reports from around the world described strange appearances ... and disappearances. The Brits had as many weird reports as anyone except the Americans (who suffered hundreds of abductions by aliens!) Can you explain the following? No one else can!

THE VANISHING CYCLIST

Liverpool. On 5 March 1970, 13-year-old David Craig set off to cycle to school. It was just half a mile and he was keen to get to his favourite lesson – French. He never arrived. The next day his cycle and his cycling cape were found. He has not been seen since. Scotland Yard refuse to discuss the number of missing children cases reported every year. Some police forces say no records are even kept. Where are all these children going?

GIRL CATCHES FIRE

Darlington. On 16 November 1979, dancer Vicky Gillon was in the toilets at a disco when she appeared to burst into flames. Her friends beat out the flames and skin grafts saved her life. Reports said that lighting a cigarette had set fire to her cotton dress. But later tests on similar dresses showed that they smouldered. They did not burst into flames. Can a human body burst into flames by itself?

PHANTOM THIEF

Norfolk. On 13 February 1974 police raced to answer a burglar alarm at a house in Kings Lynn, Norfolk. They found the house was securely locked. When they finally got inside there was a trail of footprints across the floor of an empty room ... all made by the same foot, and vanishing when they reached the far wall. There is a history of the house being haunted by a one-legged priest. As the police said, 'Why set off a burglar alarm when you can walk through walls?'

FEATHERED FIENDS ATTACK

Northumberland. On 10 August 1974 Kevin Gray was crossing the Tweed Bridge in Berwick when he was suddenly set upon ... by a flock of seagulls. Time and again they dived at him, shrieking and clawing. Kevin ran for his life. Other people reported the same problem. It was like something out of Alfred Hitchcock's film The Birds. Some animal experts believe the birds may have been defending nests built under the bridge. But seagulls are not known to attack humans. What suddenly drove them to attack Kevin?

ROY'S TEETH TURN UP, BY GUM!

Devon. In June 1976 Roy Patterson was swimming at the seaside town of Beer when his false teeth fell out and sank. Later that year he returned to the town and heard about a set of false teeth that had been washed up on the beach. He traced the finder, tried the teeth ... and discovered they were his! Amazing coincidence ... or some strange force that links a man and his teeth?

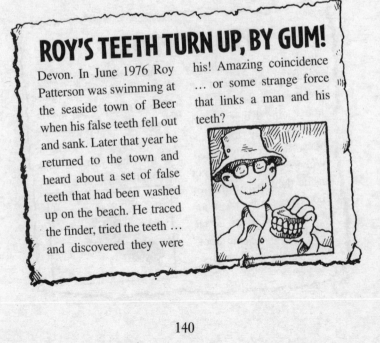

I WAS KIDNAPPED BY AN ALIEN

Glasgow. On 9 November 1979, 60-year-old forestry worker Bob Naylor was driving to work at Dechmont Hill in West Lothian when he spotted a silver spacecraft in a forest clearing. The alien craft saw him at the same time, flew across and grabbed him. Something dragged the stunned Bob back to the field where he fainted. He woke and the alien presence was gone but there were marks where legs of some craft had rested. There was also a trail across the grass where he had been dragged. Bob is a well-respected and responsible man. If he isn't lying then what actually happened to him on that lonely road?

WELSH WONDER

Anglesey, Wales. On 27 February 1977 a netball teacher, Bronwen Morris, was refereeing a game when she spotted a strange object in the sky. She hurried her pupils indoors and asked them to draw what they had seen. All the pictures showed a cigar-shaped object topped with a black dome. They can't all have imagined the same thing, can they?

141

GRUESOME FIND

Cornwall. Builders made a grisly find when they restored an attic in a Falmouth house on 20 December 1976. It was a human arm. They didn't report it but left it for the scaffolders. When the scaffolders arrived they failed to report it too and left it in the road. Finally a shocked passer-by called the police who said the mummified arm had belonged to a woman and could be anything from five to 100 years old. The arm still had a note attached – a little joke left by the builders. It said, 'In case you need a hand!' But who owned that arm, how did she die, and who killed her?

CLOSE SHAVE

London. In November 1971 a young architect decided to kill himself. He went onto the London Underground and waited for the next train. The train rushed out of the tunnel and a passenger had a moment of madness – he snatched at the emergency brake handle. An instant later the architect threw himself in front of the train. Because of the passenger's unexplained action the train stopped a fraction before it crushed the architect and his life was saved. The passenger was asked why he had pulled the emergency brake at that precise moment. He had no idea what drove him to do it. Do you believe in miracles?

BLACK PUDDING BLITZ

Derbyshire. October 1977 and Castleton pensioners survived the German blitz of World War II only to be attacked again … in their own homes! Night after night four old people's bungalows were pelted with groceries. They included bacon, tomatoes, bread, eggs and black pudding. Police were called in and the attacks stopped. But, as pensioner Mrs Edith Brampton said,

'It's weird! If someone wanted to give us presents then why didn't they just wrap them up and leave them on the doorstep?'

After the psychic Seventies the Eighties seemed much more sensible and these curious stories are not so common. Why did the Seventies see this explosion of the weird and unexplained? It's a mystery!

The Greedy Eighties

Nobody has given a name to the 1980s – yet. Maybe it should be the Greedy Eighties. The great aim is to make as much money as possible. A popular American film gives a new phrase that could be the motto of the Eighties … 'Greed is good.' In Ethiopia people are starving while the greedy westerners feed their own faces. Fortunately those awful pop music people show they are not so bad after all and 'Live Aid' concerts help the starving.

Timeline – 1980s

1980 Pop singer John Lennon of the Beatles is shot dead by a fan. If that's the action of a *fan*, then what would somebody who hates pop music do?

1981 Peaceful Britain disturbed by riots in the streets. In the boat race the Oxford boat is steered by a woman for the first time – and Oxford win! (No more nasty remarks about women drivers, please.) Princess Diana says, 'I take thee, Philip Charles Arthur George, to be my lawful wedded husband.' That's a shame – Prince Charles's name is 'Charles Philip Arthur George'. (Seconds later she makes an even bigger mistake when she says, 'I do.')

1982 Britain goes to war again over who owns the Falkland Islands. The average age of the soldiers is 19. Queen Elizabeth wakes up to find a strange man sitting on the

end of her bed – no, it's not Prince Philip, it's an intruder, Michael Fagan (who is nearly as strange). The Queen's maid walks in and exclaims, 'Bloody 'ell, ma'am! What's he doing in here?' That's what you call a *good* question.

1983 The winner of the Derby is kidnapped – the horse, that is, not the jockey. Shergar vanishes from his Irish stable. Probably ended up as tins of dog food. Mrs Thatcher elected Prime Minister again and a Liverpool woman has sextuplets – no connection.

1984 Hedgehog-flavoured crisps are invented by a pub landlord. Animal Rights protesters are furious and the idea is abandoned. To enjoy them nowadays you would have to take a packet of beef-flavoured crisps, place them on the nearest country road and wait for the first passing car to run over them.

1985 Brit inventor of the pocket calculator, Clive Sinclair, invents the C5, an electrical tricycle – then wishes he hadn't. No one wants to be seen dead in one … unless the little thing ends up under a bus in which case they *would* be seen dead in one.

1986 Halley's comet seen over Britain. Usually a sign of disaster and, sure enough, Chernobyl

Nuclear Power Station in Russia explodes. The radiation goes up in the air and the rain over Britain brings it back down. Result: radioactive sheep. (You can't eat them but they're safer than normal ones on the roads because they glow in the dark.)

1987 BBC weatherman says, 'Earlier today, apparently, a woman rang the BBC and said she heard there was a hurricane on the way. Well, if you're watching, don't worry. There isn't …' Next day the South of England is wrecked by the hurricane. You win some, you lose some. Talking of losing … the money markets in London are hit by a financial disaster – lots of people lose a lot of money.

1988 Beware of eggs! The government Health Minister, Edwina Currie, warns people that eggs often contain salmonella poison. She is right, of course. Most governments would take action to make eggs safe. Not the Brits. Worried egg–eaters stop buying eggs, egg producers complain and Mrs Currie gets the sack! This is no yolk for the people who keep getting salmonella poisoning.

1989 Television cameras allowed into parliament for the first time. Five million viewers fall asleep with excitement. A writer called

Salman Rushdie writes a book called *The Satanic Verses* – it upsets the people of Iran so much they threaten to kill him. Thousands of people rush out to buy the book (to see what all the fuss is about). They, too, fall asleep with excitement . People start to worry about Global Warming and the Ozone Layer.

The twocker's tale

The greedy Eighties were fine for those who had the power to make money. People were judged by how much they earned. It was the decade of the Young Upwardly-mobile Professional Person (yuppie). If people with money were 'successes' then people without money saw themselves as failures. And if you couldn't make money honestly then you could happily make it dishonestly. Car crime increased in the Eighties, especially amongst the young …

'What do you want to do when you leave school, Billy?' the teacher says.

He's always asking me hard questions like that. 'Dunno,' I tell him. It always upsets them when you shrug your shoulders and say, 'Dunno.'

That's when I get the lecture. 'If you work a bit harder at school you can pass your GCSEs and …'

Yeah, yeah. I've heard it all before. Me mum says she got six GCEs and look at her. On second thoughts, *don't* look at her. Her face is enough to give you nightmares.

'Where you going tonight?' she asks.

'Dunno,' I tell her.

'Just stay away from the back of the old cinema,' she says.

'Why?'

'Cos that's where the Andersons hang out,' she says.

So, what do I do? Go to the back of the old cinema, of course. Why do I do that? Any time somebody says, 'Don't!' then I just have to. That's how I ended up in here.

Now the lads that meet at the back of the cinema are sitting in a car. I can't help staring at it. Ten thousand quid's worth of car and the engine rumbling like me dad's stomach after tea. 'Like it?' Mel Anderson asks.

I just nod. 'Want to drive it?' he asks.

'Can't drive,' I tell him.

'I'll show you,' he says.

'I'm only fourteen,' I tell him.

'That old, eh?' he grins. 'I was twelve when I started.'

'Joy-riding?' I ask.

His face goes hard and he holds it close to mine. His voice is very quiet. 'We are not joy-riders, son. We don't take cars for fun. We steal cars to sell. Taking Without Owners' Consent. Twocking. Don't ever call us joy-riders. We're twockers. Got it?'

'Yes, Mel.'

'We do it for the money. Want some money? Want to be rich?'

'Yes, Mel.'

And that's how it started. They taught me to drive, then they taught me to steal. Then they taught me to sell the cars and make money. I was the richest boy in our school. I had more money than most of the teachers, I reckon.

I'm sixteen now. Two years and I was never caught. I'd still be free now if it hadn't been for Josh. I handed the car over to Josh and he paid me the money. Then he drove off and got caught by the police.

Josh talked. He told the police about me. I told them he was lying. But they found my fingerprints in the car. Hardly seems fair that, does it? I'd stolen the car and I'd got away with it.

The judge said he was sick of dealing with joy-riders. That annoyed me. I shouted and told him, 'I'm not a joy-rider. I'm a car thief. It's not a game, it's a job.'

I think that made it worse for me. He sentenced me to three years in this Young Offenders' Institute. Every night locked in a cell. Every day tormented by the bullies. Work in the gardens and the workshops. Lessons in the classrooms. And the teachers ask me, 'What do you want to be when you get out, Billy?'

Now I know what to tell them. 'A car thief.'

It wasn't only the car thieves who came to an unhappy end. In 1987 there was a change in the London money markets that cost a lot of yuppies their jobs ... and their money.

Curious crimes

Could you be a judge? It's not just a problem of finding out who committed a crime – the police do that. It's not a matter of deciding if the accused is guilty – the jury does that. No, you have to decide what to do with the criminal once he or she has been found guilty. Their sentence. In the 1980s the Government built one billion pounds' worth of new prisons to take criminals. But what did the judges do? Fill them? Or let people go? What would you do in these curious cases?

1 In 1975 two 17-year-old boys set fire to a primary school in Durham. The judge said, 'School arson must be stamped out. I am sending you to prison for four years.'

In the same week in 1975 an 18-year-old set fire to his bedroom at Harrow Public School. He caused £92,000 worth of damage. His punishment was what?

a) Four years in prison because it is the same crime.

b) Eight years in prison because the damage caused was twice as much.

c) Two years in prison because the judge felt sorry for the fire-raiser.

d) Nothing. He was set free.

(Before you answer, here is a small clue which *may* be important or which may not have affected the judge at all … you decide. The Harrow fire-raiser was a second cousin to the Queen.)

2 An American tourist, 48-year-old Josephine Carlin, had heard the old joke question, 'What does a Scotsman wear underneath his kilt?' (The answer, if you didn't know, is 'Nothing!') But, being American, she just had to find out for herself. When she visited Edinburgh in 1988 she saw the Scots guards on duty. She walked up to one and pretended to drop a coin. She bent to collect it and as she stood up she lifted his kilt! He grabbed her arm. His sergeant came and arrested her. She was found guilty of 'malicious mischief'.

What happened to her?
a) Set free and told not to be so stupid again.
b) Sent to prison for six months.
c) Fined £150 and sent to jail for one night.
d) Deported back to America and banned from visiting Britain again.

(Clue: This should *not* influence your judgement at all! Josephine Carlin was a *teacher!* What an example to set to her pupils!)

3 David Cannon was a farmer in Northern England. After 45 years of work on the land he decided to retire. There was a plot of land on his farm which would be perfect for his retirement home. He asked the council for permission to build his house there. They refused. Time after time he applied. Time after time he was refused. 'They are giving me a load of bull's droppings,' he complained, 'So I'm going to give them a load of bull's droppings.' He loaded six tons of manure onto his muck-spreader ... and sprayed the Town Hall with his smelly load. He was arrested for 'disturbing the peace.' What did the judge decide?
(Clue: The manure flew in through open windows so it covered desks and computers and staff as well as the building.)

a) He had to pay the cost of the cleaning bill.
b) He was fined £1,000.
c) He went to prison for six months.
d) He had to scrub off the manure himself.

4 A man walked into a London bank with two hand-grenades and a knife strapped to his belt. 'Gimme your cash and there'll be no trouble,' he barked at the cashier. The woman smiled and said, 'Do you have an account at this branch, sir?' The angry robber pulled a gun and snarled, 'Give me the cash or I'll use this!' Bells jangled as one of the other cashiers hit the alarm button. The robber stumbled towards the door to be met by an army of police officers. 'Don't hurt

me!' he cried. 'I've got a weak heart. I was on oxygen three days ago.' He was arrested and found guilty of armed robbery. What sentence did the judge give him?
(Clue: The robber was 74 years old. Apart from the weak heart he also had gout in the foot which had slowed his getaway.)

a) Twenty years in prison.
b) Life imprisonment (because the judge felt sorry for him and his 'life' would be less than the 20 years).
c) Suspended sentence. The man was free to go provided that he did not commit any more crimes.
d) Fined £2,000 for causing distress to the cashiers and given two weeks in prison.

5 America had crime problems too. In Florida, Mrs Vann saw a boy removing the model flamingos that decorated her lawn. She recognized the boy as Tony Salgado, the son of her neighbour, Mrs Margit Salgado. The flamingos were returned but the deputy sheriff called on Mrs Salgado to deal with the matter. What did he do?
(Clue: Tony Salgado was three years old and thought the flamingos were toys.)
a) Warned Mrs Salgado about her son's behaviour and asked her to control him in future.
b) Placed Tony Salgado under 'house arrest'. That is, he was forbidden to leave the family house at all.
c) Warned Tony to behave himself – and gave him a packet of chewing-gum.

d) Told Mrs Vann that she was making a fuss about nothing and said she was wasting police time.

6 An old woman died friendless and penniless in an old people's home. By chance police discovered that she was in fact Lady Illingworth, the widow of a millionaire. What had happened to her fortune? After a difficult investigation they discovered her niece, Baroness de Stempel, had stolen everything of value from the old lady and even forged her will before leaving her to die in the old people's home. In 1990 she was found guilty of fraud and forgery. What punishment did the judge decide on for Baroness Stempel? (Clue: A particularly cruel and sad thing was that old Lady Illingworth always wanted to be buried in her family grave, next to her husband. Because she was abandoned at the end, her body went to a council crematorium and her ashes were scattered there.)

a) Fined £10,000.
b) Released.
c) Seven years in prison.
d) Six months in prison.

Answers: **1 d)** The judge said, 'Sending you to prison would serve no useful purpose. Discharged.' The fact that the 18-year-old was a second cousin to the Queen would make no difference to a judge … would it? **2 c)** The judge was trying not to laugh when he heard the case. Still he felt he had to protect the guardsman's privacy and gave her this steep fine. Now, whenever people ask Miss Carlin, 'What does a Scotsman wear under his kilt?' she answers, 'Go and look for yourself!' **3 a)** The farmer had to pay the cleaning bill. He never got the permission he wanted, but he had a lot of satisfaction from his protest. 'The Town Hall workers should feel honoured,' he said. 'That was no ordinary manure. That was from a prize-winning herd!' The punishment did not put Mr Cannon off his smelly revenge tactics. In 1995 he was accused of repeating this sort of attack … on a bank that upset him! **4 c)** The judge decided the old man was no threat to the public and released him. The robber explained that his girlfriend was the same age and desperately needed an operation to repair her damaged hip joint. He was only stealing the money to pay for her operation. **5 b)** The three-year-old was placed under house arrest! He could not leave the house for two weeks while the sheriff's department decided what to do with him. In the end the sheriff himself apologised to Mrs Salgado and said his officer should not really have arrested a three-year-old. **6 c)** The judge said that the Baroness's treatment of her aunt was 'barbarous' and gave her a long prison sentence. Meanwhile lawyers fought another case to get back Lady Illingworth's fortune from the Baroness and give it to the people who deserved it. Some estimate that the gold, antiques and property were worth 12 million pounds. Hopefully the Baroness will not have a fortune waiting for her when she comes out of prison.

In 1936 John Langdon-Davies published a book called *A Short History of the Future*. Apart from saying, 'There will be no war in Europe in the next five years' (wrong!), he also predicted, 'Crime will be considered a disease after 1985 and will cease to exist by 1990.' (We're still waiting.)

The Nostalgic Nineties

In 1897 Queen Victoria celebrated 60 years on the throne – her Diamond Jubilee. As the 19th century drew to a close people began to celebrate by looking backwards. At the end of the 20th century it seems that Britain is doing the same thing again – looking back. In 1995 the British government, among others, organizes a celebration of the 50th anniversary of Victory in Europe Day (VE Day), when World War II ended. It is a great success and brings Brit people together as nothing has since the 1982 Falklands War.

Timeline – 1990s

1990 People riot in the streets of England. This time their excuse is that something called the Poll Tax is unfair. Mrs Thatcher takes the hint and hands over her job to John Major. The Cold War is beginning to end as the Berlin Wall is knocked down. Nelson Mandela is released from his South African prison so things are looking up.

1991 The Gulf War starts in Kuwait and British troops join the action. They fight Saddam Hussein in Iraq. Old Saddam is a bad loser and sets fire to the Kuwaiti oil wells when he loses the war (but he keeps his job).

1992 Some things never change, 1: Clever Brit inventors are creating exciting new products. A Hartlepool housewife invents floating soap using a microwave oven and a food processor on normal soap … but no one wants to manufacture it and the product sinks. Never mind. At least she tried.

1993 Some things never change, 2: Brave Brit explorers are still out to beat the world. Sir Ranulf Fiennes almost crosses the Antarctic on the longest 'unsupported' trek in polar history. On the other hand some things *do* change! He is eventually rescued by helicopter – a luxury that Captain Scott didn't have 80 years ago!

1994 The Channel Tunnel finally opens. Britain has a land link with the Continent for the first time since the Ice Age. Some Brits fear animals with rabies will cross from the continent but they are told the Channel Tunnel is animal-proof … until a French dog is found wandering 6 kilometres inside the tunnel!

1995 Fifty years since the end of World War II and Britain celebrates 50 years of peace – the Suez crisis, the Gulf War, the Falklands war, etc. don't seem to count! People start spending their cash on National Lottery tickets – even though they're only likely to win once every 28,000 years! The hottest summer for 19 years and people say things like, 'Aha! Global warming! This is the beginning of the end of the world! Doom! Doom! Doom!'

1996 The Queen celebrates her 70th birthday by announcing the divorces of two more of her children – times have certainly changed since the end of Queen Vic's reign in 1901. What *would* old Vic have said? People give up eating beef because they think humans can catch mad cow disease. However, they carry on eating treacle pudding because they

don't know about the even deadlier mad custard disease.

Slagiatt
The United States Patent Office keeps a record of all new inventions. Once you have described your invention to them no one may copy it. In 1899 the Director of that Patent Office made a bold statement …

Everything that can be invented has been invented!

This, of course was *serious* news. Inventors may as well give up … and the Director may as well look for a new job!

There was just one thing wrong with his statement.

Everything.

It was the most incredibly *stupid* statement in the history of stupid statements. (Of course, if the 21st century comes up with a *more* stupid statement, then this statement will become a new landmark in the history of stupid statements.) The 20th century has seen more new ideas than any other.

The trouble is a lot of 20th-century inventions have side-effects that no one expected. Then the inventors shrug and say, 'Seemed like a good idea at the time.' (SLAGIATT)

Which of these dodgy devices belong to the 20th century?

1 Brillo pads

Aluminium pans were popular but hard to clean. A pan salesman and his brother-in-law came up with a pad of steel wool and a bar of soap sold together. Simple idea? (So how come you didn't think of it?) It sold well in America but World War II rationing almost killed it off when it arrived in Britain.

Then Brillo had two brill ideas. First they mixed the soap in with the wool – second they began to advertise on the new Independent Television in 1955. Bingo! Unfortunately Brillo is such a powerful scourer that it can be destructive in the wrong hands. In 1995 a woman offered to help her boyfriend clean his car ... and removed some stubborn bird-droppings with a Brillo pad. She also removed a lot of the expensive paintwork. Ah, well, SLAGIATT. But was it from this century?

2 Poll tax

A 'poll tax' means a tax demanded from every adult – the same amount regardless of whether you're living in a mansion or a bedsit. A bit unfair, you might think ... and the thousands of people who rioted because of the poll tax in 1990 would agree with you. It must have SLAGIATT to Mrs Thatcher and her Conservative Party – but was it a 20th-century idea?

3 Aerosols

First invented by a Norwegian but made popular by the Americans as insect killers for their troops. (The insects carried diseases that killed even more people than the enemy bullets and bombs!) By the 1980s seven billion aerosols were being produced each year. That's when scientists accused the aerosol gases of destroying part of Earth's atmosphere – the ozone layer. The result, some say, is that harmful rays from the sun are getting through and killing humans. Ah, well, SLAGIATT.

4 Petrol-driven motor cars

A rare type of killing machine. Unlike a gun, the motor car can kill the person driving it as easily as the person who gets in its way. It murders innocent victims (like hedgehogs or low-flying crows), it causes a mental condition called 'road rage' (causing usually-sane people to use it as a hand-controlled torpedo), it gives off lead into the air (which may cause brain damage in children), it leaves unburned hydrocarbons causing smog in cities (and deaths from lung diseases, and increased asthma) and it is being blamed for global warming (where the ice caps melt and most of the world is drowned). Ah, well, SLAGIATT. But is it one of this century's?

5 Skateboards

Rather like surfboards on wheels. These lethal vehicles do for children what motor cars have done for adults … but without the pollution. In America a medical association described them as 'a new medical menace' while Brit magazine *Good Housekeeping* whinged, 'Seldom has a sport created so many fractured arms, wrists and legs, concussions and lacerations as skateboarding.' The top speed is a ridiculous 78.37 m.p.h. – the US record holder, Roger Hickey, broke 44 bones before he achieved that immense fame. Was it worth it? Ah, well, SLAGIATT.

6 Guy Fawkes' Day fireworks

It seemed like a good idea to celebrate King James's escape from the Gunpowder Plot. How did people celebrate? They lit bonfires … and, over the years, burned more houses, barns and haystacks (not to mention men, women and children) than Guy Fawkes could have managed in a hundred plots. Ask any fireman – Bonfire Night is a *bad idea*. But someone had a worse one. Add dangerous *fireworks* to the celebrations. They soon discovered one important fact – children and fireworks do not mix. Lots of little fingers, noses and ears are scattered

162

around Britain to prove it. Oh, dear, SLAGIATT! Was this a 20th-century invention?

7 Disc jockeys

Those irritating, mindless babblers who spoil good music at discos or on the radio by *interrupting*. Disc jockeys do not like *pop music*, they do not like *classical* music, in fact they don't like music at *all*. They like just one thing … the sound of their own voices. Still, someone decided that records needed to be introduced and gave the job to a disc jockey. Someone, somewhere thought it SLAGIATT. But when?

8 Eleven-plus examinations

God made children happy – teachers are paid to put a stop to that sort of nonsense. One of the best ways of making children miserable is to give them endless tests. When they fail they will be upset – and if they aren't upset enough then the teacher may shout at them until they are more upset than spilt milk.

The eleven-plus was a great invention because some children might pass it but far more children had to fail it. In the first eleven-plus exam only 2,167 could pass out of

75,000 – less than three per cent. Imagine being eleven years old and you are told you are a 'failure'. This torture is largely abolished now but … SLAGIATT. Another brilliant idea from the 20th century?

9 Bras

You may have noticed that women's chests tend to be a bit, well, wobbly. To control the wobble women had worn corsets made from whale bones – and there's not a lot of wobble in a whale bone. Then Mary Phelps Jacob instructed her maid to use two handkerchiefs and pieces of ribbon to make a suitable sling – and invented the bra.

The suffragettes welcomed the freedom from whalebone – and had a whale of a time. BUT by the 1970s the granddaughters and great-granddaughters of those World War I trendies saw the bra as a symbol of women being restricted. Some women in the 1970s burned their bras! Ah, well, SLAGIATT.

10 Machine-guns

The machine-gun is a particularly nasty weapon. The operator sits behind it and cuts down enemy soldiers like a harvester cuts down corn. A human soldier becomes an inhuman killing machine. A World War I corporal describes this feeling …

> *When the Germans were attacking they were mown down just the same as we were. They were urged on by their officers just the same as our officers were urging us on. They were coming over just like cattle. You just felt, 'You've given it to us, now we're going to give it to you,' and we were taking delight in mowing them down. Our machine-gunners had a fine time with those Lewis Machine Guns. You just couldn't miss them.*

If the inventor ever saw his machine at work did he say … SLAGIATT?

Answers: **1 Brillo pads** Yes. The pad that cleaned the car and caused £400 worth of damage was invented in 1913. The car was a Peugeot and the woman was called, believe it or not, Mercedes! She said, 'I only wanted to help.' The car-owner, Neil Anderson of Swindon, said, 'I'd better be careful what I say or she might set about me with a Brillo pad.' There are no recorded cases of assault and Brillory on police records.

2 Poll tax No. Poll taxes have been causing riots since the 14th century! You'd have thought that might have given Margaret Thatcher a bit of a clue, wouldn't you?

3 Aerosols Yes. A 1926 invention by Erik Rotheim. It was the war in the Pacific Ocean (WWII) that made the USA produce 50 million 'bug bombs' and the popularity of the aerosol was certain. In the 1970s the aerosols that used atmosphere-destroying gases were banned in the USA and Europe. But is it too late to halt the destruction of the ozone layer?

4 Petrol-driven motor car No. An 1883 invention by 27-year-old Edouard Delamare-Debouteville. (Just as well we don't name this invention after its inventor!) Still, it has made fortunes for a lot of people in the 20th century. If someone can invent a car that will drive through floods (that will be caused by global warming) then they may make another fortune in the 21st century. Rearrange the letters of 'car' and call it an 'Arc' – Noah what I mean?

5 Skateboards Yes. Young people had been riding boards on roller-skates since the 1930s but the first manufactured ones appeared in the USA in 1963. At least 20 US cities banned them from the streets. Oregon police arrested a skateboarding dog. But this suicidal hobby became popular again in 1973 when plastic wheels made the boards more 'steerable' than the old ones. It reached a peak in Britain in 1977 when cats, dogs and little old ladies were forced to run for cover as the craze swept the paving stones. Sort of crazy-paving, you might say.

6 Guy Fawkes' Day fireworks No. Fireworks themselves were first recorded in China back in AD 1103. The first Bonfire Night took place in 1607, two years after Guy Fawkes's failed plot. We're not sure if fireworks were set off then, but they were certainly being used 70 years later. A poem of 1677 says …

*Now boys with squibs and crackers play
And bonfires' blaze turns night to day.*

KABOOM!

ARGH!

7 Disc jockeys Yes. The BBC asked Compton Mackenzie to introduce some records on radio in 1927. Just before the programme was due to be broadcast Mr Mackenzie went missing. Wise move. His place was taken by his brother-in-law Christopher Stone. Unwise man – he lived to regret it. Mr Stone had the honour of being the world's first disc jockey. He died in 1965 and swore 'till his dying day that he absolutely hated being called disc jockey.' But he recorded his will on a gramophone record! (Remember, I said that they like people to hear their voices ... even after they are dead!)

8 Eleven-plus exams No. The first of these fiendish tests were set in 1893. The London School Board set the exam at the age of 11 because the school-leaving age was 12. If you passed then you would go on to Grammar School – if you failed then you'd know you had about a year to start looking for a job. The first council to abandon the eleven-plus examination was Anglesey in 1952, and it was abandoned altogether in the seventies, when most schools in Britain were 'comprehensive' – all children could go to the same schools.

9 Bras Yes. 1913 invention ... although many other people have claimed to have invented this contraption.

10 Machine-guns No. The Americans used Gatling machine guns in their Civil War in the 1860s. It was in the 20th century that these guns changed the whole idea of war. Earlier wars had been about two armies meeting and fighting, winning or losing. Now they met and stopped each other with walls of flying lead from the machine-guns. Blame the 20th century for inventing warplanes that bombed people in their homes and for nuclear bombs that did horrific damage. Don't blame it for inventing the machine-gun – just for the cruel and wasteful way it was used.

Date quiz

The 20th century has seen a lot of changes. Yet some things hardly ever change. People, for a start. Some of the things they say could have been said in any one of the 100 years. Look at these quick quotes and try to guess when they were said.

1 Slums People living in miserable conditions are described here ...

Few of the children here have ever seen a bathroom and in some homes there is not even a towel and soap. All these homes have overcrowded sleeping and living quarters; for example ten or eleven people may sleep in two beds and one cot. The living room usually measures about ten feet by nine feet and contains a gas stove, cupboard, sink and small table. The children are restricted to playing in the small yard or on the pavement of the main road.

a) 1903
b) 1933
c) 1963

2 Disasters Sometimes a shared problem brings people together as in this terrible time ...

It was nice in some ways. We talked so much more to neighbours. You had to; and what one person didn't have, you shared. At the beginning we didn't think it was going to last, and so we lit candles all over the house. But then

we began to realise it might take a long time, and we cut down. Of course you couldn't buy candles or torch batteries anywhere by then. We did run out, but we had several offers from people who helped us out.

a) 1917
b) 1941
c) 1987

3 Kids Teachers complain about children falling asleep in their classes. They usually place the blame something like this …

Children, after sitting in the cinema till eleven o'clock at night, come weary and listless to school the following morning. Many children become pilferers to get pence for admission to the show; others actually begin a downward course of crime by reason of the burglary and pickpocket scenes they have witnessed.

ZZZ
YAWN!
ZZZZ

a) 1913
b) 1943
c) 1993

4 Behaviour High unemployment is blamed for many things, including the behaviour of young people …

5 Inventions It's always hard to tell what effect a new invention will have on the world. People who try to guess are often wrong as here …

6 Fashion Tastes change but some opinions don't. This insulting advice tells women what make-up *men* want them to wear!

a)

'*Don't let him see your five-tiered trolley of make-up products. Let him think you are naturally beautiful for now.*'

a) 1937
b) 1945
c) 1995

b) Theatre Director C. B. Cochrane says:

A woman ought to use make-up so skilfully that she looks as though she wore none at all.

a) 1937
b) 1946
c) 1995

Answers: **1 c)** 1963 This report was looking at education but it also commented on the home lives of some of the children. It could still have been written in 1993. **2 c)** 1987 The friendly spirit of people recovering from a disaster is often compared with Londoners in the World War II Blitz. In fact this comment was made after the 1987 hurricane destroyed hundreds of homes in southern England. Parents may have coped with the disaster well – quite a few children grumbled about the loss of their beloved television! **3 a)** 1913 The priest who wrote this also complained that children witnessed massacres and catastrophes on the screen and it gave them nightmares. Children getting bad habits from watching films is an argument that is still going on in the 21st century. **4 b)** 1931 The headmaster of Darlington Grammar School was saying what headmasters have said for 500 years – children aren't so well behaved as they were in the 'good old days'. (The truth is they never were!) **5 c)** 1985 The inventor of the electric tricycle predicted this when he launched his battery-powered vehicle. The public disagreed with him and the petrol engine persists. No one has yet come up with a really popular successful electric vehicle. **6 a)** 1995 The *Sun* newspaper also advises men not to talk about 'how big and powerful your car is. It's guaranteed to drive a woman insane with boredom.' **b)** 1937 The *Daily Mail* also advises that a medical officer has condemned lipstick as 'repulsive'.

Epilogue

History is all about 'change'. But there has never been a century quite like the 20th century for change. There's probably been enough history in the last 100 years to fill a million books. And the exciting thing is that *you* were part of it.

In your own lifetime you'll have seen satellite television, personal computers, the Channel Tunnel and the internet. On the down side you'll have used those televisions to witness wars and disasters and crime and cruelty.

And you'll have seen that some things *never* change if you live to be a million – births and deaths, wet weekends and school dinners.

One of the major figures in the 20th century was Winston Churchill. When he was a young man he took part in a war where his troop charged the enemy with swords and lances. By the time he died countries were threatening each other with atomic bombs. That's the sort of change the 20th century has seen: the *weapons* have changed but the *people* using them haven't. They still want to kill each other to get what they want! History can be truly horrible.

As the century slipped away people spend a lot of time looking back. That's not such a bad thing – so long as we remember the horrible lessons of history and learn from them ...
• the misery of unemployment
• the suffering of loneliness – especially in old age
• the inhumanity of people at war
• the waste of valuable talent because of class, race or sex prejudice.
But humans are an unbelievably cheerful lot. Hopefully we'll also remember (and learn from) the good things of this dying century ...
• the heroic (or slightly mad) people who make breakthroughs by being the 'first'

- the power of modern communications to make everyone feel 'involved' and useful
- the opportunities we have for happiness (now we don't have to spend all the daylight hours down a mine, for instance)
- the magic of seeing the world change week by week.

The 21st century will also be about change. Change for the better or change for the worse? That really depends on you.

One day, when you are very old, someone will say to you, 'What was it like living in the 20th century?'

What will you say?